Love is the Greatest
Flex

DR. LARRY EDWARD BIRCHETT, JR.

Table of Contents

DEDICATION

FOREWORD

ACKNOWLEDGEMENT

DEDICATION

This book is dedicated to Arlene and Larry Sr., my Mother and Father, who was the first model of parental love, romantic love, and friendship that I ever experienced on the planet Earth. Specifically, my father Larry Birchett, Sr. challenged me to write this book. After he read my last published book, Interdimensional Prayer, one day he just kind of said nonchalantly that my next book should be a book on love because when he read my last book it was a book of spiritual warfare. I was literally in the beginning process of writing my next book, but I couldn't get his words out of my head. God finally shut down that book for the moment for other spiritual reasons and then God began to give me the format of this book. He told me seven chapters, an easy read, and a book on love as it pertains to His heart.

I'd also like to dedicate this book to all of my children, Larry III, Maya, Jayden, Akeem, Danisha, Zi-nei, Pocus, and Bebe. And also to my granddaughters Zoe, Anne and Gamaryia. All of you touch a place in my heart that is untouchable. There is a reservoir of love in my heart and soul for all of you that is deep and unquenchable and I love you all unconditionally. One of the greatest privileges in my life is to be considered a "dad" and a "father" in your lives.

Last but definitely not least, I'd like to also dedicate this book to my beautiful, gorgeous, funny, and amazing wife Joanna. Before I met you a Prophet told me that my "latter would be greater than my former" as it pertains to love. And oh my, was God right on point. Ever since God placed you in my life it has been one of the greatest joys in my life to love you. Your spirit is rare and your love is pure. Like Song of Solomon 3:4 says, I have found the one whom my soul loves. You are my heart in human form and I love flexing in this thing called life with you.

FOREWORD

It is a privilege and honor to not only be married to Apostle Dr. Larry Birchett, Jr. but to have this great opportunity to write the foreword for this amazing book: "Love is the Greatest Flex."

Love can be expressed in various ways. Love empowers us to defend the people we care for and the things we believe in. Love is the key component that the Lord has given us and when it is present in our lives, it enhances and expands us.

I am a firm believer that Love is the greatest flex, yes, it is! And when we understand that, it creates the atmosphere where #Lovewins. One of the most distinguishing marks of Christians is their love.

The Bible teaches us so much about Love; God has loved us with an everlasting love **(Jeremiah 31:3)**. We love, because He first loved us **(1 John 4:19)**. Jesus said, *A new commandment I give to you, that you love one another, even as I have loved you, that you also love one another. By this all men will know that you are My disciples, if you have love for one another;* **(John 13:34-35).**

Apostle Dr. Larry uses the Word of God to remind us that Love is the most powerful force. The enemy does not want us to love one another. If he can create division or animosity, he will! And once that seed is sown, that is all he needs to work.

I endorse this book; it is tied in with the Word of God and encourages us to love. We know God loves us simply because He WANTS to love us. He CHOSE to love us. He DECIDED to love us. God loves us because "God is love," and when we grasp this understanding, we will be more loving one to another, because "Love is the Greatest Flex"

Apostle Dr. Larry has given us different strategies in the book on the importance of Godly love. We know that *for God so loved the world that He gave His only begotten Son* **(John3:16a).**

Love is not taking but giving, Love is selfless not selfish. And when we truly love one another, we are representing Christ to someone.

As you read each page of this book, allow the Agape love of God to permeate your mind, body and spirit. May you be blessed with love, which is the greatest flex!

Prophetess Dr. Joanna Birchett
DHum. M.Ed.
Co-Pastor- Harvest House Restoration Center
CEO-Gospel 4 U Network

ACKNOWLEDGMENT

I'd like to thank the Holy Spirit for pulling out the grace that God has attributed and imbedded in me while I was in my mother's womb for the purpose of this book I have been inspired to aspire for my highest self in God as He continues to reveal to me and in me His purpose for my life.

I'd like to thank my gorgeous and gifted wife, Joanna, for her love and support of me via this book and everything else that God has placed in my heart. You're always there my love and it means the world to me. It's you and me to the end of time *babygirl.*

I'd like to thank my children who inspire me with their very existence and unconditional love towards me. I love you all so much and I pray that as your father that I've been the champion that every father is supposed to be for their sons and daughters.

I'd like to thank my parents Dr. Rev. Arlene Paulette Birchett and Reverend Larry Birchett, Sr. for pure love and dealing with me in love even when I didn't deserve it. I love you two so much and I'm blessed that Mom you weren't just a Mom to me you were a Mother. And Dad you weren't just a Dad to me, you were a Father. I honor you both for rearing me and my beautiful sister, Nija Birchett, in the way that we should go.

I dedicate this book to you both for being my first examples of what real love looks like. From prayers in the morning, to taking me and my sister to the movies, to church, and to theme parks. I praise God for every family trip and vacation. You guys did your best and held it down for decades for me and Nija and I Love you both.

I'd like to thank my spiritual father and mother Apostle Dr. Earl Palmer and Prophetess Dr. Maria Palmer for always being there for me and my wife, Prophetess Dr. Joanna, and for always being a source of encouragement and strength. I praise God for you both and your labor of love concerning me.

I'd like to thank my church, Harvest House Restoration Center, the greatest church in Pennsylvania, for encouraging, inspiring, and obliging me to explore what God has for me. It is an honor to be the under-shepherd of such an awesome congregation. You all are such a blessing to me.

Lastly, I'd like to thank the Holy Spirit for equipping me and helping me during the arduous process of putting this book to paper. The writing of this book was challenging because I learned that the love of God is deep, vast, and limitless. We all know that in theory but trying to express this truth on paper is another story. It wasn't an easy task to identify which parts of His love that He wanted me to put pen to paper. God I am grateful for yet another example of Your love to me in giving me what I needed to complete this project. Father God, may you get all of the glory from this body of work.

Love Is The Greatest Flex

Love is the Greatest Flex

1 Corinthians 13:13

"And now abideth faith, hope, charity, these three; but the greatest of these *is* charity."

Let me ask you a question. If an Angel showed up and told you that you can have whatever you want out of three things: the relationship/spouse of your life for the rest of your life, the best car in the world for the rest of your life, or the best figure in the world for the rest of your life. Which one would you pick? Hopefully you chose the relationship which would translate into the wife or husband of your dreams for the rest of your life. Why? Because LOVE, without a doubt, is the greatest flex beloved. What good is the car if you don't have anyone to take in that new car smell with? What good is having the finest figure in the world if there is no one that you really care about and that cares about you to appreciate it and to drool all over you?

When I use the word flex, I'm using it in the modern vernacular to mean that in modern times people put on their best clothes, drive their best car, and wear their best hairstyle, to sort of show off and show that they're doing good and feeling good. This is what the modern culture calls "flexing". You can think of it as sort of flexing your muscles. When you flex your biceps or pecs, you're showing off all the hard work that you've done behind the scenes. You're saying, *look at my nice big arms, aren't they nice?* And since that verbiage is established, I'd like to show you and explain in this brief body of work, that love should always be chosen over every other good thing that this life has to offer, because a life lived without love is no life at all.

In 1 Corinthians 13:13, Paul writes, *"So now faith, hope, and love abide, these three; but the greatest of these is love,"* Love is the greatest because **God showed us, through His Son Jesus Christ, how great His love is for us**. Therefore, through that expression from God, we know that love is the greatest. The logical progression of the three is that faith is the substance of hope which leads to love. And love is greater than the three because only love is everlasting and never-ending. As a Pastor, I have the duty and honor, however sad and unpleasant it may be at times, to conduct funerals. And one of the things that I always say to the family and those that really loved the deceased, is that even though we can't see our loved one in Heaven right now, we know that they still exist because our love for that person hasn't stopped or diminished. Love is so powerful that it even crosses the threshold of death into every other realm and dimension. I guarantee that whether some of our loved ones that has passed from this life is in Heaven or Hell, our love for them still remains. Am I right about that? It's exactly like the love that God has for us, as Paul explained in Romans, chapter eight.

Romans 8:38-39 (KJV)
*[38] For I
am persuaded, that neither death, nor life, nor angels, nor principa
lities, nor powers, nor things present, nor things to come,
[39] Nor height, nor depth, nor any other creature, shall
be able to separate us from the love of God, which
is in Christ Jesus our Lord.*

As already stated, a lot of people think that the greatest flex in life is money. A lot of people think that the greatest flex is prestige. A lot of people think that the greatest flex is notoriety but I'm here to tell you that love has always been, and it will always be the greatest flex on the planet Earth. The Bible says in **Mark 8:36:** *For what shall it profit a man, if he shall gain the whole world, and lose his own soul?* Likewise, what does it profit you to gain all the money in the world, build the biggest business, have the biggest church or ministry, be the most famous person out there, but not have someone to share it all with. Many people have found themselves in this exact scenario and this is the reason why a lot of rich people and even celebrities are depressed, on medication, hooked on illicit and illegal drugs, and some of them are even suicidal. Coincidentally, as I'm writing this book an interview with Matthew Perry, one of the stars from the hit television series 'Friends' just aired with ABC's journalist Diane Sawyer, and he divulged that at one time he used to take 55 Vicodin pills a day mixed with Xanax's, Methadone, a quart of Vodka and other substances daily just to feel okay. And I don't bring that up to shame him, but I bring it up because it has been proven over and over again that happiness fostered by wealth is an illusion. An illusion that has been presented to mankind from the beginning, but is a lie. satan started this idea in the Garden of Eden. And he even had the nerve to tempt Jesus in Matthew chapter 4, with all of the riches in the world but of course Jesus rejected him.

Matthew 4:8-11 (KJV)

[8] Again, the devil took him to a very high mountain and showed him all the kingdoms of the world and their splendor. [9] "All this I will give you," he said, "if you will bow down and worship me."

[10] Jesus said to him, "Away from me, Satan! For it is written: 'Worship the Lord your God, and serve him only.'" [11] Then the devil left him, and angels came and attended him.

At the Council of Trent, St. Thomas Aquinas, an Italian Dominican Friar and Priest described the three sources of temptation as:

- **world** -- "indifference and opposition to God's design", "empty, passing values"
- **flesh** -- "gluttony and sexual immorality, ... our corrupt inclinations, disordered passions";
- **the devil** -- "a real, personal enemy, a fallen angel, Father of Lies, who ... labours in relentless malice to twist us away from salvation";

And he said that these three sources are "implacable enemies of the soul". And if these labels and categories are correct Jesus withstood the greatest temptations to our souls that there are. The method He used was resistance. The Bible says that if you resist the devil, he shall flee.

James 4:7-8 (NKJV)

[7]Therefore submit to God. Resist the devil and he will flee from you. [8]Draw near to God and He will draw near to you. Cleanse your hands, you sinners; and purify your hearts, you double-minded.

And so we learn from the scriptures and from Jesus example that all we have to do to resist the temptation of worldliness, because satan offered Him the world, is resist and maintain a humble spirit. Jesus being God incarnate is just and so there is no way that He could sin. However, for us normal people the only motivation strong enough to keep us from failing and falling is love. I love the old song, *Love lifted me, love lifted me. When nothing else could help, love lifted me.* If we don't love God more than we love our sin we can't consider ourselves really being in love with Him.

John 14:15 (NKJV)
[15]If you love Me, you will keep My commandments.

John 14:21
Whoever has My commandments and keeps them is the one who loves Me. The one who loves Me will be loved by My Father, and I will love him and reveal Myself to him."

John 14:23
Jesus replied, "If anyone loves Me, he will keep My word. My Father will love him, and We will come to him and make Our home with him.

John 15:10
If you keep My commandments, you will remain in My love, just as I have kept My Father's commandments and remain in His love.

1 John 2:3

By this we can be sure that we have come to know Him: if we keep His commandments.

1 John 5:3

For this is the love of God, that we keep His commandments. And His commandments are not burdensome,

2 John 1:6

And this is love, that we walk according to His commandments. This is the very commandment you have heard from the beginning, that you must walk in love.

So, if you love God, do what He says and understand that drugs, money, sex, or fame will only bring you burden, pain, and depression. Love on the other hand can allow a person to be happy whether they have money, whether anybody knows their name, or whether they have completed any great accomplishment on Earth as far as the criteria that mankind usually considers to be called great accomplishments.

I remember when I was in the military, specifically the United States Army in 2008. We had an operation that was being conducted in South Dakota. One of the perks of this particular operation is that during our down time I was able to take certain members in our unit with me sightseeing. One of the places that I can remember that we were privileged to visit is called the Mount Rushmore National Memorial, located in Keystone, South Dakota. It is a mountain but far more than that it is a mountain with some of our greatest American leaders majestically carved into the side of it. Such as presidents President Lincoln, George Washington, Theodore Roosevelt and even Thomas Jefferson. Their faces are carved into the face of the mountain, surrounded by the beauty of the Black Hills of South Dakota and it is breathtaking to behold this national treasure. I was able to visit this National Monument three times and even though I was so impressed and so honored to be able to see this great national monument and human achievement, one of the only things that I could think about the whole time is that I wish Joanna, my wife, and all of my children were there to witness that great monument and experience those once in a lifetime moments with me.

This moment impressed in my spirit that the places that you go can bring you joy but without someone to share the experience with, it will never fulfill your spirit. Great moments without someone to share the experience with gets downgraded to just good moments. The moments that we relive over and over in our mind, heart, and spirit are the ones that we were able to share with another human being. This is true because we are relational beings. It's the way that God wired us and why God said concerning Adam, that it wasn't good for him to be alone. God never intended for us to be by ourselves for too long.

I know of couples that were once considered royalty to many of us and to others because they looked like they were the perfect couple. Over time some of these couples have fallen apart, most of the time because one of them has developed irreconcilable affections concerning the other. Sometimes these splits occur due to true incompatibility and irreconcilable differences maybe because of a breach of trust but sometimes it's due to emotional, mental, and relational immaturity.

And so, these individuals have decided to explore other relationships and paths in life. And I've seen these individuals go out and get in other relationships, even re-marry, and seemingly achieve everything that they felt like they were missing in the first relationship only to have those relationships not make it either. Was the problem really the other parties in these relationships or them?

Some of these people have become rich and made names for themselves, travelled the world, and have become what the world would consider successful, but they're still not happy. These individuals if you talk to them still finds all the faults in whoever their current mate is, tend to be very narcissistic and are still trying to "make something of themselves" and prove to everybody else that they're happy and got it going on.

Conversely, I've seen other couples that have been together for twenty-five, thirty, thirty-five, forty, fifty years or more. They're older now but they still come out every morning and sit on the front porch together and read the paper or share a cup of coffee. These individuals still go to the movies together and show up at functions together, holding hands nonetheless, and you know what I've noticed? I've noticed that all eyes are always on them notwithstanding their appearance, whether pretty or ugly, big, or fat, or even disabled, they are always the main attraction. Just the fact that two people that really love each other, probably color coordinated in their clothing, and looking like each other because they've been together for so long, are in the place, sharing the moment with everyone else in attendance is always the greatest flex in the room.

They are normally the most peaceful, secure, and happiest people in the room, and it draws the eyes and attention of everyone. Real love will always attract the minds and spirits of men and woman because it is originated from a place outside of this world and when it exists in this world it's one of the rarest things to witness and hence, God created us to be relational beings downloading within us the greatest and strongest magnet of all time, love. So, if you are in a relationship and real love is present, make it work. As long as you are not in a situation that is jeopardizing your health and well-being, make it work beloved. Fight for it with everything in you because you literally can't do any better than love.

Mark 10:9 (KJV)
⁹ What therefore God hath joined together, let not man put asunder.

Marital and/or romantic love is not the only type of relationships that I'm referring to when I talk about love. Some of you need to be fighting for your sons and daughters and grandsons and granddaughters. To me there is nothing cornier than a mother or father that doesn't love their children in word, deed, and action. If you fit this category, I call you corny because your kids didn't birth you, you birthed them and so your responsibility is to them, not the other way around. However, if you don't teach them what love is they will never be able to reciprocate to you and others. Which is why it baffles me when grown men and women act nonchalant towards love.

To my fathers and my mothers, it's your job to create a culture of love in your family. It's your job to set up days during the month or at least throughout the year that the family knows that they will be congregating at your house. It's your job parents to ensure that when children and even grandchildren want to stop pass that the invite and your door is always open. Parents it was or is depending on what season of life that you're in, your duty to show what healthy loving relationships look like. The phone call regiments, the birthday cards, the Thanksgiving holiday meals, the Christmas traditions, not to forget the "I love you", are all instituted by you mothers and fathers. There is no child on earth that does not like to hear that their mother and father loves them, and it can never be said enough. So be intentional about your love to your children and your sisters and brothers and your mothers and fathers. Be public about it because real love is not afraid of publicity. Jesus wasn't private about His love for us. His crucifixion was and is the most public execution of all time and He did that out of love for us. *For God so loved the world, He gave His only begotten Son. That whosoever believeth in Him shall not perish but have everlasting life.* **John 3:16.**

This is not to say that God will not bless you in private and give you some private blessings, lessons, and victories. But the limitation of the private blessing, lesson, or victory is that it stays just with you. Unless you share what God has allowed in your life no one else will be able to be blessed by it or impacted by it, good or bad.
And if that is how God intended us to operate again, He would've never said to Adam, the first man, that it wasn't good that he was alone. Also, we know that we learn from each other and overcome the enemy by the blood of Jesus and our shared experiences.

Revelations 12:11 (KJV)
And they overcome him by the blood of the Lamb, and the Word of their testimonies, and they loved not their lives unto the death.

This scripture teaches us the power of our words and Kingdom declarations as well as the power of an intense love. Whatever we say will find a way to manifest in our lives so we should be very careful in what we choose to say. Therefore, many are living an inferior life because they keep cursing themselves. But when we combine our words with biblical knowledge and start decreeing blessings and Godly things in Jesus mighty name in conjunction with applying the blood of Jesus, we will see results. On top of those things when our love for God reaches to the level that we don't care about what happens to us, even death, God will move Heaven and Earth for us.

For human beings, our greatest desire is a relationship even though our greatest need is God. It has been put in the DNA of every human being the longing for the greatest gift and experience that life can offer that is normally termed, love. And for most, not just a friendly love, but a love that can only be felt, touched, and satisfied deep within the divine sacred fires of our eternal souls. Not merely a physical or tangible fondness but an intangible and spiritual longing and desire that transcends all else and would cause a person to forsake all else to be with and obtain it. Who would not want to experience a love like this? It is not a man's or woman's appearance or title that will woo you. It will be his or her mind and spirit that will court yours. And like **Song of Solomon 3:4** says you will say *"I have found the one whom my soul loves."* And this person will speak in a manner that only your heart can hear. The rest of the world will go quiet when you are together, and your souls will dance together, transcending the physical into the spiritual. Once again, who would not want to experience a love like this?

Some of you have never heard of love being spiritual but it is. **Because love is not just a feeling—love is an action, a manifestation of emotion, a choice, a moment of faith where we decide, with everything in us, to be with and for that person or idea of that person no matter what.**

Have you ever heard someone tell another person that "I would move the mountains for you."? If you have any amount of life experience in conjunction with just a little bit of emotional maturity you would know that these words if they were said with a genuine heart, came from a deep place. Has anyone ever said anything like this to you and meant it? Or maybe this is something that you have said to another person? If either of these scenarios are true, then you already know that the substance embodying these kinds of words is what we would normally call love.

Dashrath Manjhi, also known as the 'Mountain Man' did it for real. He split a mountain for the woman that he loved. Dashrath lives in Gehlour, a small village in India. His story is that one day his wife fell off of a cliff. He tried everything but could not maneuver his wife through the mountains and valleys to get her to the doctor in time; subsequently, she died. Dashrath became so determined after that heart breaking and life altering event to make sure that no one else would ever have to endure what he just went through. So, with strong determination, and people calling him things like 'psychopath', for 22 years Dashrath broke up and did demolition to so many stones in the mountains that he paved a 400 feet long and 30 feet wide road that connected the village to the nearby city. His only motive was to give people of his village access to medical services so that nobody would lose a loved one like he did. Love was his motivation and without love fueling him this road that has saved countless of lives since then would've never been formed.

Love is the strongest force on earth and is made from the fabric of God's essence, because God is Love. If you don't have love, know love, or show love you don't know God because literally everything that God has done and created concerning you and me was motivated by love. The force of love is what made God create the world and us. Let's look at what John had to say about the relationship of God and His love.

1 John 4:7-8 (KJV)

Beloved, let us love one another for love is of God and everyone that loveth is born of God and knoweth God. He that loveth not knoweth not God for God is love.

The greatest force in all of existence is Love. Nations, empires, and governments have gone to war in the name of love. Nations, empires, and governments have also ceased wars in the name of love. We have all heard the stories of Cleopatra and Mark Antony who decided that after their conquest together against Rome was defeated that to die together would be the best option due to the fact that they couldn't bear to live in this life without each other. Or how about the story of Romeo and Juliet? Or to bring it more current, have you ever heard of Prince Harry and Meghan Markle? Prince Harry loves his wife Meghan so much that he has renounced his royal title and position, left the palace, and has gone into the world to live as a commoner with the woman of his dreams. That's love.

The greatest art that this world has ever known has been birthed out of love. Much of our greatest music, literature, ideas, and ideals have all been birthed out of the strongest force on Earth, love. The most purchased, printed, and distributed book of all time is a love story. Did you know that? The name of this piece of work is called, 'The Holy Bible'. And in 1 Corinthians 13:3 of this best-selling love story, the Apostle Paul says, ***"Three things will last forever: faith, hope, and love-and the greatest of these is love."***

You may ask yourself why anyone would classify the Bible as a love story. It truly is beloved. The whole premise of the Bible, which is the Word of God, is to give the whole account from creation to the present, and to the future of how and why God sent his Son, Jesus Christ of Nazareth, to die for all of humanity in order that we could all be reconciled back to him.

The most popular scripture in the Bible is **John 3:16** which states,

*For God so **loved** the world that He gave His only begotten Son. That whosover believeth in Him shall not perish, but have everlasting life.*

A lot of people know the verse and even recite the verse but only to communicate that Jesus came to die. And even though it is good to know that Jesus was born to die so that we might live forever with our Father who is in Heaven. It becomes an even more powerful fact when we realize that God provided Jesus in our place because he **loved** us. For God so **loved** the world is how the scripture starts. And one of the devil's chief attacks against the mind of a person that is not convinced that anyone loves them let alone God is that God does not love them. One of the purposes of this book is to kill that lie and let you know that God does love you beloved and He loved you so much that He gave His only begotten Son Jesus, in protest against the consequences of His own law to make sure that you and I could live with Him eternally. God loved us so much that He sent Jesus, His only begotten Son, as a ransom for our sinful flesh to be a redeemer of our souls.

Many people tune out on the subject of love as soon as God is introduced, but this is a mistake. Because true love can only be understood and interpreted by God and what we know about Him because God is love and God is the creator of it. If you want to be successful in love beloved, include the creator of it, God, Jehovah Elohim, in it and watch your love flourish. It's important to know that God is love as John taught us this fact in 1 John 4:7,8 to gives us a glimpse into His divine identity. His identity is important because we are His children and as it is in the natural, so it is in the spiritual. Since we are His children, our spiritual DNA is supposed to contain the same propensity for love as His does.

The reason why the world is so messed up with lust, confusion, anger, and murder is because humanity has lost touch with its true identity. We were made in God's image, but this information has been tampered with and added to.

Genesis 1:27 (KJV)
So God created mankind in his own image, in the image of God he created them; male and female he created them.

A person who doesn't know who they came from, especially if the person in question is the father, will undoubtedly struggle with identity and abandonment issues. The trauma that the mind keeps rehearsing in the form of thoughts of rejection, abandonment, and questions about identity, will eventually pierce the soul of a person which will in turn injure the spirit of the person because the spirit is contained within the soul. It is the enemy's job to lie to us to make us feel unwanted, not special, and to make us develop low self-esteem. Which is why we must be careful to always marshal our thoughts. We have to cast down every imagination that exalts itself against the knowledge of God.

2 Corinthians 10:5 (KJV)
Casting down imaginations, and every high thing that exalteth itself against the knowledge of God, and bringing into captivity every thought to the obedience of Christ;

If you don't know who you are satan can tell you who you are. And of course, he will never tell you the truth. He will lie to you or tell you half-truths to confuse and derail you. The problem with that is identity attached to Lies or Non-Truth always lead to Perversion. Identity attached to Truth leads to Conversion. And this is why we have so many people in our generation with a perverted view of who they are. Their identity has been attached to a perverted image of God.

If you as a man, think that God is a woman or highly feminine, like a lot of men and women do, then you won't think that there is anything wrong with a man that acts highly feminine or worse has given up all aspects of masculinity to be a woman in their own mind and heart. This is why the trans movement and homosexual movement is growing and growing because of identity issues. For some of them it's not that they love themselves it is that they have been deceived as to who they are and what they were really meant to be. The role of the man has been downplayed and downgraded so much that real men get ridiculed and vilified for being men. If your voice is too deep, you have an anger problem. If you exemplify the gift of leadership that every man has been born with too much, you have a control problem and if you're not careful they will try to shame you as a man and counsel your God given gifts to lead and be in charge away. It's the same thing that happened to Adam in the Garden of Eden when he started following his wife instead of leading his wife and got all of us in trouble. The devil's playbook has never changed. But what did satan probably play with to get Adam to follow and fall? He probably used Adam's love for Eve to make him join her in her mistake so that she wouldn't have to face the consequences alone.

If something like this really happened to Adam, I think that it is a shame because real love always makes people, places, and things better. When you choose to love someone, you are choosing to make them better. Your so-called love should make them better. If Adam would've had the benefit of reading this book before following Eve in "eating the forbidden fruit" he would've understood that Eve didn't love him in the way that he deserved to be love. Because real love would never put the other party of said love in jeopardy or harm's way. Adam should've been able to look at the whole situation objectively and say, *hey if this woman really cared and loved me like she says she do, she would've never put me in a situation where the Creator, God Elohim, might kill me or be very angry with me. Besides I did tell her not to do it.*

Which leads me to my next point. Which is Self-Love. The whole concept of love from one human to another was obviously new, so I'm not being too hard on Adam because eventually some man and woman would've have done the same thing that Adam and Eve did. However, Self-Love is an important requirement to be able to love another person in the right way. Why? How can you love me with a full and robust mature love when you don't even love and care about yourself? I love my wife Joanna, with everything within me, but I will not follow her to the gates of hell if she should choose to start serving the devil because I love myself. Get it?

A lot of people are trying to prove their love by following sinful and unhealthy examples of love just to so called, "be in love". Self-love, however, will always alert you to the fact that you deserve better when these situations occur. Self-love is directly connected to self-worth and when either is being treaded on something should arise within you beloved to allow you to say, *I'm not going to allow you to bring me down in the eyes of God or otherwise because of your lack of devotion to God and discipline in life.* That's called self-love. And when you operate like this a person without it will try to manipulate you by calling you self-righteous or holier than thou, but if God is the person that you care about pleasing the most this won't move you. Tell them I'm not going to smoke crack with you just to have a so-called boyfriend or girlfriend. Tell them I'm not going to look the other way when I know that you have another boyfriend or girlfriend just to have a so-called boyfriend, girlfriend, husband, or wife. Tell them I'm not going to allow you to abuse me mentally or physically, just so that I can have a so-called relationship. Tell them I'm not going to allow you to trash my credit simply because you're not wise enough to allow someone else to handle your finances. I'm not going to get obese and unhealthy with you simply because you don't value the merits of healthy living and working out. You get the point beloved? Okay, let's move on.

Love, which is more than a feeling or an emotion, has caused men to kill other men, and women to kill other women, and on the flip side, love has also caused others to live for the welfare and benefit of other men and women as well. I have members in Harvest House Restoration Center, the church that I pastor in Carlisle, PA that have faced the gates of death numerous times but have been motivated and inspired to live because of their love for their children. There are countless stories of people that held on to a fragment of their life until a certain family member finally made it to their hospital room from overseas or from some sort of deployment, or something similar. During the writing of this book in October of 2022, there was a tourist named Dustan Jackson who was kidnapped by a cab driver in Mexico. The story goes that he and his wife were at the airport, and he wanted some chewing tobacco. The first store, a gas station, that the driver took him to was out of chewing tobacco. The driver said that he knew another place to get some. And that's when the kidnap occurred.

"I'll never forget that feeling," Jackson said. "It was the scariest feeling in the entire world." Jackson said that the driver told him he knew a place where they could go, a grocery store. But that's when things got much worse. "I get out, and I'm like 'Ok,' and then as I'm walking and it's boom, lights out and the next thing I know I'm waking up in a ditch," he said.
Jackson said he was attacked by a group of men armed with a machete. They used the machete to cut up his foot. "They went to cut my Achilles tendon, and they missed and instead of hitting it,

they hit the bottom of my foot and then my foot just flapped around," Jackson said. " They were trying to cut all my tendons and leave me for dead."
He was left in the dark in the middle of nowhere. Jackson, who doesn't know Spanish, stumbled around for hours screaming for help. At one point he said even the cops turned him away, before he said he crawled under a tarp to die.

"I don't know what kind of power it is when they talk about the mental strength that you have as a human being, because at this point however long I was laying there, pretty much just waiting to die, something inside of me, that strength came to me and said 'You've got family, you've got kids. Get up,'" Jackson said.
Jackson did just that, eventually coming upon a female police officer who stopped to help him. She eventually got him back to the airport where he said he met another guardian angel. A woman from Africa whose flight was canceled offered to help him. This whole story was transcribed from Fox11 based out of California.

For somebody that's reading this book right now, God is encouraging you to hold on just like Jackson did, because that specific person that you love is counting on you to hang in there. God is encouraging you to hold on because that loved one that you've been praying for is going to come around. God is encouraging you to hold on because He's not finished with you yet. Love lifted Dustan up and out of that tarp and if you tap into it, love will lift you up as well beloved. Think about your children before you just give up. Some of you have wives or husbands that need you to live the life that God has planned for them. So, crawl out of that hole victimization. You are not a victim, you are a victor. Yes, like what happened to Dustan, some bad things have happened to you but there is nothing that you can go through that can break the genuine bond of love.
Love is the bond that can never be broken. Love is patient and kind as well as longsuffering according to 1 Corinthians 13. As a matter of fact in that same chapter it says that "love never fails". So, endure and be longsuffering for the one that you really love and while you are doing this, make sure that you're doing it for the right reasons. **When Love Is Your Motivation, There Is No Fear.**

"Wherever God's love is, there is no fear, because God's perfect love drives out fear."
1 John 4:18 (NCV)

A lot of people think the opposite of fear is faith. But this is not true. The opposite of fear is love. Love is the force that moves against fear. When love comes in the front door of your heart, fear goes out the back door. You can't be afraid and loving at the same time—not with real love. When you have real love—God's love—then you don't have to fear. Parents will put their lives at risk to protect their families because they love their babies. That's why you'll see a parent quickly step in front of a child when bullets are reigning all round. It's not fear that makes parents or a husband or wife do something like that for the other, it's love. People don't run into burning buildings to rescue children because of faith. They do it because of love. The litmus test to figuring out if love is your motivation is the absence of fear.

"Wherever God's love is, there is no fear, because God's perfect love drives out fear"
(1 John 4:18 NCV)

Now, please understand that there is a difference between a person that loves you and the person that is just a beneficiary. Some people seem to love you until they get what they want from you and then they conveniently change all up. Newsflash, they never loved you in the first place. A lot of times this is one of those things that you only learn through experience. The key is to grow though what you go through. Because not one of our experiences are accidental. God allows us to go through a myriad of experiences to evolve, grow, become enhanced, and more mature. And the prayer to pray after we gain this life enhancing wisdom, is for discernment to know the difference between those that truly love us and those that are there to manipulate us.
Jesus knew this and operated under these principles. We remember in Matthew 26:25 when Jesus called Judas out in front of all of the disciples.

²⁰ Now when the even was come, he sat down with the twelve.
²¹ And as they did eat, he said, Verily I say unto you, that one of you shall betray me.
²² And they were exceeding sorrowful, and began every one of them to say unto him, Lord, is it I?
²³ And he answered and said, He that dippeth his hand with me in the dish, the same shall betray me.
²⁴ The Son of man goeth as it is written of him: but woe unto that man by whom the Son of man is betrayed! it had been good for that man if he had not been born.
²⁵ Then Judas, which betrayed him, answered and said, Master, is it I? He said unto him, Thou hast said.

Matthew 26:20-26 (KJV)

I preached a message one time entitled, "Lord, Show Me My Judas!". I believe it's necessary to know the character and spirit of the people that are in our inner circle and outer circle of influence. Obviously, Jesus did as well. He called Judas out in front of everyone for history's sake. I believe that Jesus, being God in the flesh, knew that the history books, namely the New Testament would be written about Him and route to the Cross. And so, He had to let it be known that no one could deceive Him, but instead He tolerated certain people knowing that they were necessary to get to where He was destined to go anyway. Someone had to betray Him, right? Why not Judas. And even then, He still couldn't be captured because in **John 18:6** when they came up to Him in the Garden of Gethsemane to arrest Him, they asked Him if He was Jesus. He said, "I Am!" And they all fell back. Jesus just stood there chilling until He decided to break the ice and again ask them, *"Who is it you want?"* "Jesus of Nazareth," they said.

But the point that I'm trying to make in all of this is that Jesus knew who truly loved Him and who didn't. Jesus knew that Judas was just a Beneficiary with a lot of potential. Judas was the one that got mad at the way that they were handling the money. He was mad at the woman with the Alabaster Box of perfume for what in his small mind was a waste of good revenue earning potential. Judas obviously disagreed with the way Jesus was running the "ministry". And so, he sought to betray Him. I would surmise that Judas felt that he was being underpaid and undervalued for His services with Jesus and the disciples and so he defected.

Love doesn't keep score and doesn't feel undermined. Love doesn't keep a record of wrongs and is never in competition with the person or persons that they love. Judas obviously didn't love Jesus because he was guilty of all of these things.

DR. LARRY BIRCHETT, JR.

The Highest Form of Love

"The highest form of love is to be the protector **of another person's solitude.**" - **Rainer Maria Rilke**

Greater love has no one than this, than to lay down one's life for his friends.

John 15:13(NKJV)

I heard a story from a very prominent radio pastor that he heard from his old pastor many years before he shared it with his radio audience. The story is about two mountain goats. Two mountain goats lived on a very high and robust mountain. One day these two mountain goats found themselves on a very narrow trail that went up and down the mountain but was on the outer side of the mountain and on one side was sure death because they would've fell off of the mountain and on the other side was the actual mountain so of course it wasn't an option either. The two mountain goats were at an impasse because they both met head on as one was ascending the mountain and the other was descending the mountain. The question is what happened? Is there any way that the two mountain goats can get through this situation alive or not? Before you continue to read this chapter, look up for a minute and think about the answer to this question and then turn back to the book and continue reading beloved.

When this question was asked at a pastors conference in Philadelphia one of the pastors yelled out, "One mountain goat has to throw the other mountain goat off of the mountain!" All of the pastors had a good laugh at that because it was believed that the pastor was just having fun....we hope...lol. However, Pastor Jenkins went on to explain that unfortunately, that is the response and thought process of many. Too many of us think that we have to destroy anybody that stands in our way. Too many of us think that anybody that disagrees with us is our enemy or is a bad person. But the truth of the matter is that most of the time this is not the case. The truth of the matter is that we all are at different moments of progression in regards to our life experiences, maturity, and purpose.

We are all in process. And sometimes the process requires us to go up the mountain or as the world would say you will find yourself "all the way up". But sometimes the process will require us to go down that mountain too. Meaning that sometimes we have to tone it down. Sometimes we have to go backwards so that we can go frontwards again, just like driving a car.

But the answer to how the two mountain goats can survive is that one of them would have to lay down. One of the mountain goats would have to allow the other one to step over them or even possibly step on them so that they can get pass the other and then both could arise and resume their inevitable purpose and course of life.

Most of the time we are all on different paths. But when we choose to love another person or even a group of people we choose to allow them to occupy the same path that we are on. The key is to respect the path, purpose, and direction of another person because these things are directed and in some cases allowed by God to get us to our "expected end" according to Jeremiah 29:11 which basically is eluding to what we call purpose.

The one mountain goat acquiescing to the other mountain goat is a picture of selflessness. One of the highest qualities of love is Selflessness. I guarantee you that the person that you think embodied love the most in your life exhibited this value the most in your life. This could be your Mother, who stayed up with you all night when you were young to nurse you in your sickness and still went to work to earn money to pay the bills. Or your Father, who took off from work just to see your basketball or baseball or football game. Or your Grandmother, Grandfather, Aunt, Uncle, or someone else. I think you get the picture. It could even be a husband or a wife but I guarantee that this person selflessness to you has put them into an untouchable category even if the relationship has soured.

This is because the highest and greatest form of love is unconditional love. This is the type of love that God has for us and it's called agape love. Eros love, which is sensual and sexual love may bring a lot of pleasure but it alone won't cause another person to lay down their life for them. "Agape" is one of several Greek words for love. When the word "agape" is used in the Bible, it refers to a pure, willful, sacrificial love that intentionally desires another's highest good.

We often use the word love in different contexts and meanings. We say, "I love fried chicken" and "I love you" sometimes in the same sentence. As a pastor, when I hear someone doing this in our church I always use the opportunity to correct them. I say something to the effect of, "You don't love fried chicken, you like fried chicken." Which is normally accompanied by a brief moment of silence and thought and then laughter as they say, "Yes, I like fried chicken, not love fried chicken." It's a moment of learning and I've only had one person that corrected me back and say, "No Pastor, I'm ashamed to admit it but I love fried chicken." I'm still praying for her.

Our love for a significant other, a favorite food, and a friend are all different (hopefully). However, English doesn't lend itself well to making these distinctions.

I'm glad to report that the Greek language used in the Bible does in fact make those distinctions. Even though the various Greek words for love are all translated into the same English word in most instances, they held different meanings for Greek-speaking readers.

The highest form of love, is called Agape love. "Agape love" differs from other types of love in the Bible. It is the highest and purest form of love. It is a love of choice, not just out of attraction or obligation. This differentiation can be helpful for us to think about what love means, especially in discussing the highest form of love, agape love. Jesus went to the cross for our sins by choice. It was

His love for us that compelled Him to do it. Agape love is beautifully described in **1 Corinthians 13**.

1 Corinthians 13 (NKJV)

¹ Though I speak with the tongues of men and of angels, but have not love, I have become sounding brass or a clanging cymbal. ² And though I have the gift of prophecy, and understand all mysteries and all knowledge, and though I have all faith, so that I could remove mountains, but have not love, I am nothing. ³ And though I bestow all my goods to feed the poor, and though I give my body [a] to be burned, but have not love, it profits me nothing.
⁴ Love suffers long and is kind; love does not envy; love does not parade itself, is not [b] puffed up; ⁵ does not behave rudely, does not seek its own, is not provoked, [c] thinks no evil; ⁶ does not rejoice in iniquity, but rejoices in the truth; ⁷ bears all things, believes all things, hopes all things, endures all things.
⁸ Love never fails. But whether there are prophecies, they will fail; whether there are tongues, they will cease; whether there is knowledge, it will vanish away. ⁹ For we know in part and we prophesy in part. ¹⁰ But when that which is [d] perfect has come, then that which is in part will be done away.
¹¹ When I was a child, I spoke as a child, I understood as a child, I thought as a child; but when I became a man, I put away childish things. ¹² For now we see in a mirror, dimly, but then face to face. Now I know in part, but then I shall know just as I also am known. ¹³ And now abide faith, hope, love, these three; but the greatest of these is love.

Agape love is a sacrificial love that unites and heals. It is the love of God that we see through the cross of Jesus Christ. This love saves and restores humanity in the face of sin and death.

"Greater love has no one than this, that someone lay down his life for his friends." **(John 15:13)**

I repeat, Agape love is a love of choice, not out of attraction or obligation. This is the type of love that Jesus Christ displayed on the cross for us as he took our place for the sin that separated us from God's grace. Jesus went to that cross by choice not by obligation. It's the same reason that God didn't make us robots. He could've made us in a way that we're forced to love Him. But forced love is not real love and so that's why we will always have freedom of choice as it pertains to freewill and it's the reason why once saved, always saved is not true because many people decide to leave people that they love every day. Just because you start with God don't mean that you will finish with Him. Just ask Judas.

You don't get a diploma because you enroll. You get the diploma because you finish. And that's what agape love is all about. God will love us unconditionally from now to eternity. The question is will you continue to love Him? The word "agape" is used more than 200 times throughout the New Testament, with the most use in the book of 1 John. One of these scriptures being **1 John 4:7-8**, as I already eluded to in the first chapter of this book.

Types of Love

British writer, Anglican lay theologian, and one of the most famous writers and minds of any time, Clive Staples Lewis, who is most commonly known as C. S. Lewis identified four types of love in the Bible in Greek. Though sources such as *Psychology Today* identify seven types of Greek words for love. I'm just going to focus on the four most commonly identified.

Storge

Storge might also be called affection and relates to the empathetic bond that normally exists in what we would call familial love. To be more specific, this is the type of love that a parent would have for their child or that you would have for someone in your family. This word isn't actually used in the Bible, but the concept is there. Storge is based on familiarity. A person will love their family regardless of whether they are the type of people or person that they would be drawn to otherwise. To be honest, family members often have nothing in common except familiarity and blood.

Storge is a comfortable affection that can be taken for granted but can also be very powerful because the people that we extend this kind of love to, normally have been divinely selected by God, regardless of whether we like them or not. In the New Testament, the negative form of storge is used twice. Astorgos means "devoid of natural or instinctive affection, without affection to kindred."

Eros

Eros is another word that doesn't appear in the Bible, though it plays a major role in a lot of Old Testament problems. It is a romantic love. The word was also used as the name of the Greek God of love, Eros (the Romans called him "Cupid"). By the New Testament times, this word had become so debased by the culture that it is not used even once in the entire new Testament.

Eros encompasses sexual and romantic love and is the root word of the English word "erotic." Lovers, for example, are often completely preoccupied with one another, filled with eros.

Eros is often associated with sexual desire and lust, but desire and lust for your wife or your husband is a good kind of eros. So it can be a good thing in a marriage relationship when accompanied and bolstered by other kinds of love.

Philia

Philia is friendship love. This is the root of the word Philadelphia, where I was born and raised, which actually means city of brotherly love. Philia is a word that is actually used in the Bible. As C. S. Lewis wrote in his book, The Four Loves, "To the Ancients, Friendship seemed the happiest and most fully human of all loves." Philia occurs from bonding over similar interests. Whereas lovers are both preoccupied with each other, friends are both preoccupied with the same things. Friends, of course, care about one another, but it is similar interests that attract them to one another. "Philia" is the opposite of "phobia," literally meaning that those experiencing philia are drawn to one another.

Philia is often overlooked in modern culture but is exhorted in the Bible. In Romans 12:10, Paul urges the believers to be devoted to one another in brotherly *philia*.

Romans 12:10 (KJV)

<u>10</u> Be kindly affectioned one to another with brotherly love; in honor preferring one another;

Philia can be strongly associated with *agape* as well. In John 15:13, Jesus said there is no greater agape (love) than laying down one's life for one's friends.

Agape

Agape could be defined and is sometimes translated in certain translations of the Bible as charity. However, we often think of charity nowadays as giving away money or things, which doesn't encompass all of what *agape* is about. *Agape* love is unconcerned with the self and concerned with the greatest good of another. *Agape* isn't born just out of emotions, feelings, familiarity, or attraction but from the will and as a choice. Which leads me to explain that love is a choice. We don't fall in love as movies and fairytales try to depict, we choose to love. *Agape* requires faithfulness, commitment, and sacrifice without expecting anything in return.

This is the type of love the Bible speaks about the most. The New Testament references *agape* over 200 times.

The Christian journey begins with the recognition that you are unconditionally, irrevocably, ridiculously loved by God just as you are. Whoever you are, wherever you've been, whatever you've done in the course of your life, you are already loved and accepted. This is the Agape love of God. The highest form of love. An unconditional love that God Himself has for us.

The greatest love of all is Agape love and that's the kind of love that God has for us. So, to be clear, please understand and know that you will never be loved any more than you are right now by Elohim Yahweh, the name or attribute of God, identifying Him as the Creator. God is love and He created you and I and He loves us because He is our Father and we are His children. Hence, we can't earn more love, but we should know that God does in fact love us as we are, and we can't do things to make Him love us any more than he already loves us. However, this doesn't mean that we can't do things that pleases Him or displease Him.

1 Thessalonians 2:4 ESV

But just as we have been approved by God to be entrusted with the gospel, so we speak, not to please man, but to please God who tests our hearts.

We can never be more loved than we are right now but our hearts are constantly being weighed by God concerning every action, non-action, thought, or deed. Remember, it was God that told Cain

Genesis 4:3-7 (KJV)

3 And in process of time it came to pass, that Cain brought of the fruit of the ground an offering unto the LORD.
4 And Abel, he also brought of the firstlings of his flock and of the fat thereof. And the LORD had respect unto Abel and to his offering:
5 But unto Cain and to his offering he had not respect. And Cain was very wroth, and his countenance fell.
6 And the LORD said unto Cain, Why art thou wroth? and why is thy countenance fallen?
7 If thou doest well, shalt thou not be accepted? and if thou doest not well, sin lieth at the door. And unto thee shall be his desire, and thou shalt rule over him.

So, as we see from the Cain and Abel sequence of events, it is clear that even though He never stops loving us, there are some things that we do that pleases God and there are some things that we do that God is clearly not pleased with. In the Cain and Abel story "Cain" symbolizes faith that doesn't have love combined with it. What good is faith without love? On the other hand, "Abel" stands for charity - a love of one's neighbor. Charity, which could be translated as love, is the brother or sister of faith; they are supposed to work together, shoulder to shoulder. When faith (Cain) isn't working alongside charity (Abel), it becomes harsh, and destructive.

And that's why we have to watch doing "spiritual" work(s) in Jesus name with the wrong spirit. One of the most damaging things in the Kingdom of Christ is people operating with angry, bitter, and un-Christ like spirits. I am known for telling my leadership team at Harvest House Restoration Center that you cannot have a bad day. Some people has misinterpreted my sentiments to mean that Christians don't have bad days. But this is not the spirit of my directives to the men and women of God that graciously serve with my wife and I at HHRC.

The spirit behind my directions and directives is that if the things that are going on in your life is so heavy that you can't still show grace and operate in grace to those that God has called us to serve, then stay home. We as a local church and we as a kingdom at large cannot afford to offend people away from the love of God and the truth of His Word. We should love on everyone who comes through our doors and we should love on everyone that God leads us to serve. And for those of us that can't find that love in our hearts for the people of God and minister unto them with this love in our hearts, we can at least serve with grace.

In my grandmother's day every church was filled with parishioners because people believed in coming to church. It was a generational tradition handed down from one set of God fearing parents to another. But slowly over time, something called "church hurt" crept in the vernacular of people who had been hurt by "church people" or the operations of the church. This "church hurt" is the primary reason or excuse as to why these same people don't attend anyone's church anymore. Not to mention that we live in a digital age full of technology to include the computer, tablet, or cellphone. So, this is another excuse to be utilized by those who choose to watch someone's church service online.

These reasons and more add up to people not going into the church building. And unlike our grandmother's and grandfather's day, many churches are struggling to consistently fill the pews. Therefore, when people actually come into the church building they should be walking into the most loving atmosphere on Earth. The place where God lives. The place where His praises and worship reigns and has been perfected. A place of faith, the actual house of God on Earth.

But again, what good is faith without love? Remember, Cain symbolized faith. He was a farmer and farming requires faith. Cain rose up and slew his brother Abel, signifying that when faith and love are not operating together one is going to slay the other. Faith extinguished charity in the case of Cain and Abel. Why? Because faith that is not driven by an underlying love of the neighbor will come out to be harsh and unforgiving. And a person that has faith that is not balanced out by love will try to stamp out love because it is seen as a threat to real faith.

What Cain didn't understand and what people who operate with the spirit of Cain don't understand is that you can't break the laws of God in the name of God and expect God to accept it and be happy with you.

John 15:10-14 (KJV)

[10]If ye keep my commandments, ye shall abide in my love; even as I have kept my Father's commandments, and abide in his love.
[11]These things have I spoken unto you, that my joy might remain in you, and that your joy might be full.
[12]This is my commandment, That ye love one another, as I have loved you.
[13] Greater love hath no man than this, that a man lay down his life for his friends.
[14]Ye are my friends, if ye do whatsoever I command you.

Cain was supposed to be willing to lay his life down for Abel not kill him. The greatest love is that which you are willing to die for not the other way around. Jesus, loved us so much that He came and died for our sins so that we may be reconciled to God and have eternal life with Him.

Besides, we have the benefit of history. The mind of God is contained in His Ten Commandments which came later so Cain was not held to them as strictly as those that came after Moses had published them and made every believer accountable. However, we have the luxury of knowing the Ten Commandments and all of the rest of the commandments given to God's people through Moses and hence we know His mindset on certain things by what He told us and still tells us not to do.

For example, Cain's offering was rejected due to the fact that God was clearly delineating what He determined an appropriate sacrifice was to be in His eyes. God was setting the precedent that only the blood from an unblemished sacrifice would suffice in any type of atonement or sacrifice as unto Him. Vegetables such as leeks, onions, and lettuce and tomatoes wasn't going to cut it.

Not only was Cain's offering being rejected at that moment but he was being rejected due to the sinful character that he was displaying and the egregious breach of ethical behavior he displayed in breaking the future commandment that says, "Thou shall not covet" which Cain clearly was doing regarding God's acceptance of Abel's gift as opposed to his. And then, the most obvious failure to adhere to the moral code of God for Cain was "Thou shall not kill" one which again was not published yet, but I am sure was verbally communicated through Adam to every other living creature especially before the fall. Well, let's just say that Cain must've misunderstood that one and he definitely was not abiding in love because he was abiding in anger and jealousy due to the fact that God respected Abel's gift and not his. And just like the scripture says in **John 15:11** he lost his joy.

One of the reasons that many of us are walking around depressed is because we constantly break God's commandments. The joy of the Lord comes from having joy in God and everything connected to God. Meaning that we should love God and the things of God so much that we wouldn't dare upset God because we want His presence to always be with us. The scriptures say earlier in **John 15 verse 7**, that *if you abide in me and my words abide in you, you shall ask what you will and it shall be done unto you.*

I recently had a discussion with one of my sons. He's been dating a young woman for a few years now. He is a young man of God that already has his Bachelor's Degree and has at least two careers going on at the same time that he's always working every day. I had a conversation with him about this young woman because for Christian men, we don't date just to pass the time, we date to marry. The courting of a woman is not random it's intentional and for a purpose. And my comment to him was if she is not the one then it is an injustice to keep her on the hook if you know that you're not going to make her your wife one day.

He responded that he did in fact love this young woman and that he is going to propose one day, but then he gave me this long list of things that he had to accomplish first and then things that she had to accomplish before they would ever tie the knot. His response made me question his genuine love for her. I explained to him that true love doesn't wait for everything to be perfect. Because true love doesn't care about perfection. **It isn't found by chasing perfection. Because perfection isn't real. As a matter of fact a perfect marriage is just two imperfect people who refuse to give up on each other.**

Love and perfection are two different things. *Love* is real. Finding someone who will drive you crazy, but still make your life wonderful—*that's real.* Learning someone's inner fears, discovering what makes them laugh, finally working up the courage to kiss them—*that's real.* That's what dating and what love are supposed to be about: finding a person whose mind and heart connect with yours in strange, fun, new, and flawed ways. Finding something real, something beautiful, rather than perfect.

Two people in love would want to ensure that they are with their person in a real and meaningful way even during the lean times. Love doesn't care about how rich a person is or the size of their house. A person that loves you wants to be with you even if you don't have these things and would love to experience the thrill of the relationship that is in pursuit of building a better life.

"You know when you're in love when you can't fall asleep because reality is finally better than your dreams." — **Dr. Seuss**

True love simply is. It exists and cannot be thwarted by the cares of this life. Not to say that love is always easy but once it exists it is eternal. And my last comments to him on the issue is that you don't have to wait until you and her have it all together to express your never ending love and affection for her. I encouraged him to examine his heart and if she is the one make it official.

And to qualify my encouragement to my son, please understand that my son at the time of this discussion was a very grown man, college graduate, living on his own, taking care of himself, car, etc. He wasn't a teenager trying to achieve all of these things, he had already done these things but he wanted more. And that makes me so proud. I'm proud of my son and I'm even prouder to be his father.

However, in this generation, due to the advancement of computers and technology, we skip past the butterflies, the nervous dinners, and the awkward should-we-kiss-or-not moments. We don't get to know people, really *know* them. Know the way their nose crinkles when they laugh, what gets them fired up, what makes them cry, the way they like their eggs, their favorite quote, or their favorite movie.

We don't take the time to understand the inner workings of one another's minds, the quirks, the interactions that make the relationship truly special. **We see each other's bodies before we know each other's hearts.** And so we hurry to the most physically intimate part of the relationship before we even know the other person. Then we frantically work backwards, trying to make up for all that we've lost. Notwithstanding that sex before marriage is a sin for God fearing, Bible believing people, sex is not a temporary act. **Sex denotes permanence. When you have sex with someone your body is making a promise to them even if you are not. Soul**

ties is well known and widely talked about. But few people discuss the physical nature of it.

Physical soul ties are formed during sexual intercourse. When you have sex, your body releases oxytocin, which is also known as "the bonding hormone," which links you to your partner. Emotional soul ties form between two people with common feelings, including love. And this is why a lot of people continue to sleep with people that they know that they have no future with. They do this because of the physical and spiritual bond that has been developed by sex.

There are four kinds of soul ties: marriage, business, sex, and friendship. And people stay in each of these quadrants, even in negative situations, because of the soul ties that has been developed with the other person. If you're in an abusive marriage (physical, mental, verbal) or with an unfaithful partner it's okay to break that tie. If you're in a damaging or corrupt business agreement you can break that tie. If you're having sex outside of the tenets of God's will (fornication or adultery), break that tie. If you're in a toxic friendship, and yes It should also be known that friendships can be just as toxic as a romantic relationship, you need to break that tie. It should also be known that these relationships can be platonic as well and still fall into a category of soul tie.

And to get back to my son, as I walked away from him I started thinking about my own life. When I first met my wife Joanna, we never wanted to be apart. We loved being in each other's company and we tried our best, even as God-fearing people to do just that. She had her own house and I had mine but we spent as much of the day together as we could.

I was still an active duty officer during those days. And when we first met I was still enrolled in my Graduate program at Duquesne University of the Holy Spirit trying to obtain a Master of Science degree in Leadership and Business Ethics. I can remember that on some of those days when I had to go to class she would drive in the car with me for hours from Philadelphia to get to class. I would give her a kiss and then go to class and she would stay out in the car until

I finished my classes. I would then come out and we would be so happy that we were reunited once again. And then we'd drive all of the way back to Philly together. We couldn't get enough of each other we were so in love and I praise God that we are still like that today decades later.

My point in writing this memory is that if you do not want to spend time with your so called significant other, than you better keep looking for a person that you do want to spend time with. Especially if you are in the beginning of your relationship. The beginning of your relationship is supposed to be one of the most exciting parts of your relationship because everything is brand new. And this comment is to the non-married not the married. Because if you're married it doesn't matter what you feel, because you have already made your vows before men and the Lord and you might have to ask God to help your mind and feelings line up with His Word on the subject of honoring your vows and what love in a marriage is supposed to look like.

Too many people give up on love and subsequently marriage because of their feelings. But I'm here to let you know that **feelings ain't facts**. And I meant to use the word ain't. If you keep allowing your feelings to rule you, you're going to get your feelings hurt. I don't always feel like going to work, but it doesn't mean that I'm not going to go. Why? Because my feelings can be wrong and plenty of the times it is and I have to make my feelings line up with reality. And in the case of love and marriage you have to make your feelings line up with what God says about these things.

In marriage, God says:

Matthew 19:6 (KJV)

⁶What therefore God hath joined together, let no man put asunder.

So, if God put you guys together find a way to get yourselves together, because God hasn't changed His mind about you and your spouse. Stick it out and love each other in the way that you vowed that you would.

The funny thing about the Cain and Abel story is that Cain's actions did not change God's mind or His choice. And even though he killed Abel God still didn't accept his offering. Which leads me to the next and probably greatest flex about God's love is that His love is loyal. One of the most beautiful and underrated things about God's love is that His love is loyal. Unlike the characteristics of most humans, God's love can't be shaken. He will never cheat on us and give our love to another. God's love for us is permanent and cannot be bribed away or bullied away or intimidated away no matter what the circumstances may be. Isn't that awesome?

In 1 Corinthians 13:13, Paul writes, **"So now faith, hope, and love abide, these three; but the greatest of these is love,"** which teaches us that love is more important than faith or hope. My faith is in a God of love not a theory or concept or just mere hope. The child in Liberia that is made to kill at the age of 11 has faith in the current warlord or in his guns but faith in these things are without merit and will amount to nothing. The only thing that makes faith, the substance of things hoped for and the evidence of things not seen is love.

I can have faith in my wife and the vows that she made to me on our wedding day but if she really doesn't love me, my faith is not going to mean anything. If she does love me but her love is not loyal, like God's love for me, then it's not going to make a difference. Love is what makes the difference in every equation. Love is what makes the difference is every scenario. Love is what makes the difference in every family, relationship, or ideal.

John 15:10-14 (KJV)
*10If ye keep my commandments, ye shall abide in my love; even as I have kept my Father's commandments, and abide in his love.
11These things have I spoken unto you, that my joy might remain in you, and that your joy might be full.*

12This is my commandment, That ye love one another, as I have loved you.
¹³ Greater love hath no man than this, that a man lay down his life for his friends.
14Ye are my friends, if ye do whatsoever I command you.

These are the literal words of Jesus in John chapter 15. And Jesus is instructing us to love one another. This is not a commandment of Moses verse 12 lets us know that this is a commandment of Jesus. Jesus didn't suggest that we should love, He commanded us to love each other as He loves us. How did and does He love us? He loves us unconditionally, He loves us loyally, and He loves us eternally.

As I stated before the ancient Greeks had more than a dozen words for what we translate as the word "love." This book is not a discourse on the Greek language but I will give a few more words and definitions that pertains to love because the term love is used in many different ways and it's important to know that there are differences.

Ludus, the Greek word for playful love, was thought to be the lighter side of loving, engaged by children or in childlike play between casual acquaintances, and was seen as one of the delights of being in society. I wanted to make sure that I put this type of love in our discussion because I have counseled many people especially couples that have come to me under the pretense of romantic love or even Agape love, that was only at the level of playful love, at best.

Many times people get stuck in relationships because they've made the mistake of thinking that the early love and love interests in their lives is mature love and that it has to be the final and eternal love that most of us long for. There are many people who have married their high school sweetheart and it has worked out and turned out to be a lifelong lasting love. But there are just as many people or more that have made the same choice and are miserable or divorced. Just because you have history with a person doesn't mean that you have a future with that person. We should go to God over every person in our lives to see if God has placed them there for a season or a lifetime.

Truth is that you can never make it right with the wrong person. And most of the time the people that we were in Junior High School or High School is not the person that we're going to be at in our 30's, 40's, and 50's. And if emotional maturity, physical maturity, spiritual maturity, and a big onus on allowing the other party the flexibility to grow are not hallmarks of these kind of relationships, truth is they will never last. It takes time to figure out if a person is just a very good friend, which is the ludus or philia love that we've been discussing, or the love of your life, which would be in the agape love category. And even though ludus and philia and even eros love, which of course is a sin before marriage; are fun, they won't fuel and sustain a covenanted marriage relationship for a lifetime.

The greatest love is the love that you can't live without. The one that you would give your life for almost without thinking. The love that most parents have for their children would fall in this category notwithstanding the love that a husband is supposed to have for his wife and vice versa.

The other part of this particular conversation is that sometimes even if two parties are really and genuinely in love and right for each other, if you are too young and are not fully living the values of the Holy Bible and walking in the spirit of Jesus Christ, you can damage the love to the point of no return. This happened to me which is probably why I am so passionate about love, the "real love" that Mary J. Blige used to sing about, the kind that is divine at its essence, the greatest gift that God has ever given to man. And I am so grateful that God gave me the grace of a second chance to experience real love in the institution of marriage in meeting my gorgeous and beautiful wife, Joanna.

I won't lie and say that I've never loved before, because my wife and I met each other in our 30's, we both had multiple kids already and a history. But I will say that I've never loved anyone as maturely and completely as I do Joanna. I know this because I've never had the empathy that I have for another person's feelings and

I've never cared for another person's heart, outside of my children and my parents, more than I do for hers, right now. In the past, even when love was present and I really cared romantically for a woman I would still selfishly act on the temptations and indiscretions that every man is tempted with. But when I was faced with those same temptations in my relationship with her, it was the thought of her broken heart, along with my vow to God to never again disrespect His gift to me in this life in the form of a wife, not just girlfriend, who really loves me, that stopped me.

See, if love and romance was the only thing that we had to worry about in this life we'd probably be okay. But that's not the case. This life is also about temptation. It's about failure. It's about weakness. It's also about sin. It's about getting back up again after we make mistakes. Sin and mistakes are two different things by the way. Because God knows that we're human and are going to make mistakes. And I've made plenty of mistakes, that I've learned from. But a sin is when we know that things are wrong but we go and do it anyway. And I've done my share of that as well of which I have paid the price and have the receipt to prove it.

It is said that experience is the best teacher, but the truth is that the Holy Spirit is the best teacher. Because when the Holy Spirit is on the scene He will stop you from making the wrong choices and lead you into all truth. However, if the Holy Spirit is silent on a matter, the next best thing is a person with more experience than you. It's good to learn from experience but it's even better to learn from another person's experience. If you're the smartest person in the room, you're in the wrong room. If you're the most traveled person in the room, find another room. If there is no person in the room that you can glean from or learn from, seek an additional room.

Jeremiah 29:13 (NKJV)

13 And you will seek Me and find Me, when you search for Me with all your heart.

To put it plainly, because I dislike when people write books like this and hypocritically act like they're the second coming of Christ, was always perfect, and never made mistakes in their lives. I have to admit that I failed at love and marriage the first time around and a lot of it was due to immaturity and inexperience. I blame nobody else but myself because the responsibility always falls on the man, the God ordained head, which means that I was supposed to be the leader. The key to leading a successful Christian family is to lead with the love of God. Love is the greatest flex in marriage and it makes all of the difference. Love is about vulnerability not control, it costs you something, which is why it covers a multitude of sins. I didn't understand these things fully back then even though I thought I knew what love was and that I was doing okay.

There are only two things that we can do that covers sin. They are:

1. Loving God's people deeply and passionately.
2. Leading people to Salvation through Jesus Christ.

James 5:20

Let him know that he who turns a sinner from the error of his way will save a soul from death and cover a multitude of sins.

1 Peter 4:8

And above all things have fervent love for one another, for "love will cover a multitude of sins."

A lot of people confuse the principle of loving one another with giving money to cover their sin. Because there are translations that say *have charity one to another, for charity covereth a multitude of sin.* However, this is being taken out of context because the word charity that has been substituted for love is not referring to charitable contributions, even though love could require the physical giving of money or other things. It is actually referring to fervent, loyal, passionate, and selfless love.

However, I was not always operating with the integrity that I should have been operating with, because I had not yet developed the character of the man of God that I would later develop into later in my life. I was always a young man that loved God because I was raised in church, my father was a Pastor when I was young and my mom was an awesome woman of God that sang and ministered and everything else. And I was following God for the most part but imagine being with one person since you were 17 as I was and 14 as my first wife was. I grew up with her and my integrity meter was not yet full so because of my lack of character and disrespect for the gift of love that only God can ordain, create, and allow, I did things that damaged the trust in that relationship at certain points which led to an embarrassing divorce. How can you love somebody fully and correctly at 14 and 17 when you barely know what love is yourself? At the end of the relationship, we were in our 30's, I was Minister Larry and fully operating in the church but we didn't have the skills to overcome the spirits of bitterness and resentment that had crept into our relationship.

So, because of my life experiences and life failures, when I engage in Pre-Marital Counseling now, I am always on the lookout for the lack of life experience and experiences in the candidates for marriage. Even though I am a Pastor I don't believe that a person should marry the very first person that they've ever been in a relationship with, unless it is truly a God ordained thing. The first time a person feels the power of the gift of love it can be so intense that a person can lose themselves in it. Especially a teenager or very young person. And what happens is that because the force that surrounds love is so strong and unyielding, a young person can continue to direct that love in a direction or to a person that is not worthy or compatible to the kind of love that God built you to give or receive as it pertains to marriage.

What can happen in these instances is that you will find yourself in a relationship that you're not happy in but you'll stay because of history. And to add insult to injury you will marry the person because of the same reason. You should always choose happiness over history, especially when the signs are telling you to. Again, this is for the non-married. The married have a different criteria to choose from in this discussion because once you say I do and take those vows, in the eyes of God you are one with the other person and your skillset should then be focused on maintaining and watering the garden of love that exists between you and your spouse.

I'm not promoting sin and sexual experiences outside of marriage. But I am promoting the fact that I believe that a person should not be a novice in at least getting to know enough friends from the opposite sex and have courted enough people. How do you know the difference between a controlling person and a loving person without life experiences? How do you know what kind of communication skills work best with your emotional makeup? What type of Conflict Resolution skills do you have and which ones do you need to develop and work on? No matter who you are, only time can reveal what your love language is in a romantic relationship. These things can only be learned by actual life experience. The lack of any of these things can cause good and promising relationships to fail.

On the other hand when we are talking about friendship level love. Hear me clearly. You may only get three real friends your entire life. I'm talking about friends that you played with in the sandbox at the playground. The vernacular on the street calls them day ones, or ride or dies, always there no matter what type of friends. You should do everything possible to keep these kind of people in your circle. The love of a good friend is worth more than all the gold in China beloved.

Pragma, mature, realistic love, was considered the ground of enduring relationships between mates, family members, and others one considered essential. This kind of love involved compromise, commitment, and beyond "falling" in love, the effort to "stand" in love.

Philautia, or self-love, was thought to be natural and essentially good as grounding the individual in self-awareness, though it could descend into narcissism and self-centeredness, if it wasn't balanced in relationship to concern for the needs of others.

54

But, I want to stick a pin in this conversation right here because everyone's self-love language could be and probably is different from another person's self-love.

My self-love language is showing up for me. Respecting me. Validating me. Creating space. Healing in all forms. Knowing that God loves me. Forgiveness. Self-Forgiveness. Self-consistency. Authenticity. Genuineness. Self-honesty. Choosing peace. And choosing me.

Lastly, for this chapter, the deepest, most complex, and most demanding type of love, according to the Greeks, was *agape,* selfless, self-giving, empathetic love, extended to all people, whether family members or distant strangers. Later translated into Latin as *caritas,* the origin of our word "charity," this is the kind of love of which Paul speaks in **1 Corinthians 13 (MSG)**:

*"If I speak with human eloquence and angelic ecstasy but don't love, I'm nothing but the creaking of a rusty gate...no matter what I say, what I believe, and what I do, I'm bankrupt without love. Love never gives up. Love cares more for others than for self. Love doesn't want what it doesn't have. Love doesn't strut, doesn't have a swelled head, doesn't force itself on others, doesn't always say 'me first,' doesn't fly off the handle, doesn't keep score of the sins of others, doesn't revel when others grovel, takes pleasure in the flowering of truth, puts up with anything; trusts God always, always looks for the best, never looks back, but keeps going to the end. Love never dies....until that completeness (when we can see as God sees), we have three things to do to lead us toward that consummation: trust steadily in God, hope unswervingly, and love extravagantly. And the best of the three is love." (**The Message,** Eugene Peterson)*

One of the most freeing things that ever happened to me was when I realized that God will always love me no matter what I do. The times when I was sinning and I didn't realize it, God loved me through it. The times when I was wretched in my sin on purpose and intentionally and God still hasn't stop loving me. And I know that He has enough love waiting for me in the future for all of my future failures and imperfections. That's agape love beloved.

I know how far from perfect I am, and how inferior my way of loving has been to God's way of loving so far. I'm pretty sure that's true of most of us, because we are only human.
Nevertheless, God has planted within me and within us a longing to love and to be loved, in ways great and small, personal and communal, and I believe God expects us to keep growing in our capacity to experience and to share love in all its varieties. But especially in the capacity for agape, the greatest of these.

Holy Scripture and the teachings of Jesus and all who came after Him call us to strive for that ideal, even if on this side of the mortal journey we will inevitably fall short of perfection.

Agape, unconditional, self-giving, empathetic love, is what we all most need, to love one another, as we are so dearly loved by the One who created us, Who accompanies us, and Who inspires us on our way.

Love is Loyal

Love is when he gives you a piece of your soul, that you never
knew was missing.

Torquiato Tasso

Proverbs 3:3-4 (MSG)

*Don't lose your grip on **Love** and **Loyal**ty. Tie them around your
neck; carve their initials on your heart. Earn a reputation for
living well in God's eyes and the eyes of the people.*

Once there was a blind woman. She was very beautiful but she
was blind. She thought that she would never find true love because
of her visual impairment. However, one day a very handsome man
took interest in her. He didn't care that she was blind, he loved her
for her. She didn't have to ask for anything because he would do
and provide for her before she asked for it. He didn't care if she
couldn't see he was ready to be her eyes and ears and take of her
every need for the rest of her life.

The man loved her so much that he finally acted on it and asked the
blind woman to marry him. She said that the only way that she
would marry is if she could see because she didn't think that it was
fair for someone to have to take care of her for the rest of her life.
The man tried repeatedly to marry the blind woman but she
maintained her conviction of waiting for an eye donor match to get
the unique and special surgery that would allow her to see the person
that she would marry. The match that would suffice for her
replacement would be rare. Doctors said the probability of finding
a donor match was one in a million.

The gentleman did not give up hope and kept praying for a miracle because the woman had promised to marry him once the donor match happened and she could see. One day the miracle happened and the woman went in for the surgery.

After the surgery the man was excited and presented himself to his fiancé. He asked her if she was still going to marry him. To his chagrin she said that she couldn't because she now saw that he too was blind. The man was devastated but finally conceded to her wishes and gave her a kiss and left her with a letter.

When the newly healed woman finally looked at the letter it read, "Please take care of my eyes, they were given in love. The last sight that I saw when they were mine, was of the most beautiful woman I've ever seen, which is you. May you find everything that you're looking for in this life. I don't regret a thing. God bless."

Unless we look at a person and see the beauty in that person you can't contribute anything to that person. The man in this story saw the best in the blind woman and did not care about her limitations. He saw the best in her. Too many of us critique people and things that we don't contribute to. But he decided to contribute to the woman of his dreams and make her better. That's what love is all about. It's about making the other person better.

I led with this story in this chapter because not everybody's "I love you" really means I love you. The man who gave up his eyes to the woman he loved, in spite of her handicaps, words hit different. His "I love you and want to be with you forever" was different. He meant that he had found the one that his soul needed in his life and he didn't care about anything except for being with her. To crave a person's presence instead of their body is the purest form of intimacy.

My wife and I have a plaque above our bed with this scripture on it:

I have found the one whom my soul loves

– Songs of Solomon 3:4.

And it means that I will be with her through the good times and the bad times, sickness and health, for richer or poorer, to death do we part. My "I love you" to my wife is different than a high school or college fling, it's the real thing. When my wife was going through some physical ailments and we couldn't be together intimately for a period of time, I didn't go out and have sex with someone else. I still couldn't wait to come to her and talk about the day and listen to her concerns and sit down and eat together and share a laugh or two with her. When I was active duty and had to go away for weeks at a time or longer, I didn't have a "work wife" or a "side jawn" that I pleasured my flesh with. I never found another woman's house to go and spend my time at. She is my peace and I am hers and I love spending time with her.

By the way, the people and things that bring you the most peace should be the people and things that you spend the most time around. If you're spending the most of your time around people that you're beefing with or that you have a toxic relationship with, you only have yourself to blame.

I want to use this moment to segue into the conversation of singles looking to be married. The man that gave his eyes up for the woman that turned out to be superficial didn't know that she wasn't as beautiful on the inside as he thought she was on the outside. Which leads me to one of the most serious points of learning in this whole body of work beloved. That point being, **do it God's way.**

When I was growing up, I have to admit that some of the mistakes that I made was because I thought I knew better than my parents, my Pastor, even God on some issues. And now that I'm in my fifties all I do is chuckle at the thought. God's design for marital intimacy, sexual and spiritual, is to only be experienced in marriage. And my parents and others told me these type of things constantly. However, in my narcissism, I decided to do what I thought was best for me. I followed my own rules and was working off of my inadequate checklist.

But God gave us a roadmap to marriage. A checklist of what kind of person we should marry to how and why. Too many of us skip all of the steps that lead to marriage and go straight to sex and wonder why our relationships don't work out. Just because the sex is good doesn't mean that she won't leave you as soon as she discovers that you're just as blind as she used to be. Let that sink in beloved.

Doing it God's way means not having sex until you're married. Where do we find this at? We find it in the Ten Commandments. God cared about these ten commandments so much that there are two complete sets of ten commandments in the Bible. A lot of people don't know that. We find them in Exodus 20:2-17 and Deuteronomy 5:6-21. In addition, Leviticus 19 contains a partial set of the Ten Commandments as well, and in Exodus 34:10-26 is sometimes called a ritual decalogue.

To get straight to the point, it is in the Ten Commandments where we are given the command, "Thou shall not commit Fornication". Another scripture says , "Thou shall not commit Adultery." Fornication is defined as sex before or without being married. Adultery is sex or sexual relations with any other person than your own spouse.

God didn't put this in the Bible to punish us. He put it in the Bible to protect us. To my ladies, how are you going to know if that man loves you for you or for the treasure that God gave you between your legs if it has never been denied from that man for a considerable amount of time that the Bible commands, until you reach the altar? Many people don't get married for love, they get married just to have a steady sex partner that they don't have to work hard to sleep with or feel guilty about after the deed is done.

So, the danger in that is that if the man or woman, because it goes both ways, threatens to leave you because you won't lay down with him or her, they don't love you and you are definitely not their soulmate. If they can't wait before the marriage, then who is to say that they will wait within the marriage, when the procreation activities seem to dwindle? Who's to say that they have the love of

God, or at least the discipline to not please their flesh and won't step out on you and be with someone else when you can't physically perform? Or even worse, what happens if you get Cancer or some other type of disease that makes you a shell of what you were and they're still healthy? Have they demonstrated to you that they are with you for you? That they will be there until death do you part, through sickness and health, good times and bad times, richer or poorer, until you take your last breath. Have they demonstrated this to you? This is one of the ways that God has delineated that a person will demonstrate that kind of love before the "I do's". Don't blame God is you didn't or don't hold the person to that standard beloved.

Number one, God invented the institution of marriage and so only He has the right to define it. Marriage is a Godly covenanted union between a man and a woman of betrothal to each other. The key word is covenant. Marriage is a divine covenant not just a human contract. The thing that makes it divine is because the agreement is signed by God. God declared that it was not good for man to be alone in the book of Genesis and He put Adam to sleep. Adam had been carrying around Eve in him the whole time but he didn't know it. He was all one within himself but he didn't know it because everything else that was around him in creation wasn't.

The horses and lions and everything else found mates to unite to and become one with in every way. However, the Bible in Genesis 2:20 said that Adam must've been trying to do the same thing.

Genesis 2:18-25 (NKJV)

[18]*And the LORD God said, "It is not good that man should be alone; I will make him a helper comparable to him."* [19]*Out of the ground the LORD God formed every beast of the field and every bird of the air, and brought them to Adam to see what he would call them. And whatever Adam called each living creature, that was its name.* [20]*So Adam gave names to all cattle, to the birds*

of the air, and to every beast of the field. But for Adam there was

not found a helper comparable to him.

[21]And the LORD God caused a deep sleep to fall on Adam, and

he slept; and He took one of his ribs, and closed up the flesh in its

place. [22]Then the rib which the LORD God had taken from man He

made into a woman, and He brought her to the man.

[23]And Adam said:

"This is now bone of my bones

And flesh of my flesh;

She shall be called Woman,

Because she was taken out of Man."

[24]Therefore a man shall leave his father and mother and be joined

to his wife, and they shall become one flesh.

[25]And they were both naked, the man and his wife, and were

not ashamed.

Adam must've been looking for someone else to connect to in the same way that the animals, birds, and bees were connecting. But what he didn't realize is that when God said, *"Let us make man in our image...",* man was created as a self-contained unit, much higher than any animal, bird, fish, or otherwise. **Eve was inside of Adam the whole time but God had to put Adam to sleep to get her out of him.**

Men, when we find our wives they should fill up the part of our soul that was made just for them anyway. The Bible says to the man, in **Proverbs 18:22 NKJV**. *He who finds a **wife** finds a good thing,*

And obtains favor from the LORD. When the right man hooks up with the right woman it is the manifestation of the covenant that God has already ordained before the man and woman were ever born. Remember the scripture says, *"He who God has put together…"*.

To all of the Adam's out there, the reason why you're hunting so much for your wife is because you haven't found your Eve yet. This is the reason why some of you men are not faithful. It's because you have not met your Eve. God put it in every man to look for that one woman that "does it for them" in every way. Once you "find" your Eve you won't want anyone else because your Eve will fill up every vacancy that you have in your soul, body, and spirit.

Now, the question is how can you find your wife if you're spending your time with every woman who will give you the time of day or worse sleeping with women who were not designed to fill you up internally? Answer is that you won't. It's like trying to put a square peg into a round hole, it simply won't fit. On top of that, all of the guidelines, rules and regulations that God, the Creator of the institution of marriage, put out concerning marriage needs to be followed as well. Let's look at a brief history on how humans went about getting married from Old Testament days.

Many of the marriages mentioned in the Bible were arranged marriages in which the parents were involved in choosing a mate for their children. The practice of arranged marriage varied greatly from one family and one community to another. However, many cultures have practiced arranged marriages from the earliest times. For example, Abraham commanded his servant to find a wife for his son, Isaac (Genesis 24). The servant found a potential wife for Isaac, Rebekah, but it is plain that Rebekah was given some choice regarding whether she accepted the offer (verses 57-58).

We see from Rebekah's responses that she possessed many Godly traits, and she was clearly God's choice for Isaac. But that doesn't mean that all arranged marriages in those days were done in such a godly and submissive manner. However, this was clearly the proper way that it was to be done in those days by God's people. Notice that if you read in Genesis 24, Abraham made his servant put his hand under his thigh, as a sign of covenant that his servant would not select a woman that was not Godly and suitable for his son, Isaac. If that was the case all of the way back then, why do we think that we can marry an unsaved man or woman today and be in the will of God, for one thing, and two have a successful marriage?

Later, we see that Rebekah's son Jacob found a woman he loved and made a deal with her father, Laban, to work seven years in exchange for Rachel in marriage (Genesis 29). Though the marriage was arranged and Laban deceived his nephew Jacob, Rachel and Jacob appear to have both desired the arrangement. Unlike many depictions of cavemen knocking women in the head with the billyclub and dragging them to their caves, men and women came to some kind of agreement to marry or be married. Somewhere in there is a choice, which is appropriate in the discussion of love, because **without the ability to choose, real love can't exist.**

So, a trusted servant was sent by Isaac's father, Abraham, to find a suitable bride from his own people because he did not want Isaac to take a wife from among the heathen Canaanites. Which again promotes the will of God concerning marriage for His people. God's desire is for us to be equally yoked to each other.

"This means **these individuals should be compatible, they're able to agree on most things, and that their values are aligned**. This is also true in secular relationships, but biblically speaking in 2 **Corinthians 6:14** it says *'that we must not be unevenly yoked together with those who do not believe.'*

The Bible illustration of a yoke is taken from the huge wooden or metal clamp that is placed on the neck of the oxen, horses, or cattle to keep them line with each other. This is important when these animals are grazing. It is special because it keeps all of the animals in step and in order.

When the animals are not equally yoked, they are not working together to get the task done but working at odds with each other. **If you don't have the same beliefs, values, or even morals, you will**

be working against each other in your marriage not with each other. The Bible says it better in the book of Amos:

Amos 3:3 (KJV)

How can two walk together unless they are agreed?

This doesn't mean just that a person believes in God and His Son Jesus Christ, it means that you guys are on the same level spiritually. It means that you both love each other equally. If this is the case then you will never have to apologize to your spouse for spending all Sunday morning and possibly an occasional Sunday evening in the house of God. Because if they have the same level of love they will most likely be in the house with you.

When I was looking for my wife I wasn't looking for a woman that just claimed that they were a believer. I was looking for a woman whose behavior revealed what she believed. I praise God that I can be praying in the house or in the car or in an actual service, and God will get so good to me that I start speaking in my heavenly language. And praise God as soon as I start speaking in my heavenly tongues, I can be assured that my gorgeous and anointed wife will instantly start speaking in her heavenly tongues as well. Before I know it, we are bombarding the gates of Hell with fire straight from Heaven and I am more powerful because God has given me my eternal prayer partner. We are equally yoked, and value prayer in the same way and know that we are stronger together. And we know this because it is a biblical principle. Check out these next three passages respectively.

Deuteronomy 32:30; Joshua 23:10; Isaiah 30:17

[30] How could one have chased a thousand,
and two have put ten thousand to flight,
unless their Rock ᶳhad sold them,
and the LORD had given them up?

[10] ᴸOne man of you puts to flight a thousand, since it is the LORD y our God ᵘwho fights for you, just as he promised you.

¹⁷ A thousand shall flee at the threat of one;
at the threat of five you shall flee,
till you are left
like a flagstaff on the top of a mountain,
like a signal on a hill.

But let's not digress. The practice of arranged marriages was continued even in America and many other cultures well into the 1900s. Even today, in orthodox Jewish, Islamic, and Hindu families, arranged marriages are observed. The Bible is silent on this issue. However, the Bible does outline what a godly mate should be. For the Christian, marriage, whether or not it is arranged, is to be only to another person who is in the faith. The most important relationship that any of us have is our personal relationship with the Lord Jesus Christ. The spouse we choose should be one who has his/her focus on walking in obedience to God's Word and who seeks to live so that his or her life brings glory to God

1 Corinthians 10:31 (KJV)

³¹ Whether therefore ye eat, or drink, or whatsoever ye do, do all to the glory of God.

On this subject, I personally tell my sons and daughters, and I have five handsome sons and three beautiful daughters, that there are three requirements that any potential suitor must fulfill to possibly be put in consideration as a serious mate. These requirements are:

1. They must love God more than they love you.
2. Besides God, they must never put anything before you. And I mean anything.
3. They should know their spiritual gift(s) and be active in their pursuit of spiritual purity and service.

So, unlike Western marriages that often include much dating prior to a marriage, ancient Jewish custom included a much more reserved practice that usually included an attraction between the man and woman, an agreement between their two families, a dowry given to the wife's family, and a seven-day wedding celebration. The Jewish custom of betrothal made premarital sexual activity less likely, and divorce occurred less frequently.

To summarize our little history lesson on how people came together for the purpose of marriage according to history, arranged marriages were standard in ancient times, The Old Testament is full of examples. And it's good to know that the practice of arranged marriage arose from a strong sense of family and fidelity that often helped provide a stronger commitment to the marriage covenant. However, many marriages in the Bible were based on a formal arrangement in which both the man and the woman desired to be married.

Now, the correct paradigm of values to be held concerning the priorities of life should be:

1. God First
2. Family
3. Ministry

And in that order. A lot of people come into my office and try to hit me with the, "I'm married to the ministry" phrase. And I always immediately correct them and say, "No, you are married to your wife" or "No, you are married to your husband". It sounds good but it is not Godly and unbiblical. In the book of Timothy it teaches us that if we can't rule our houses well then we shouldn't try to lead anything in God's church. So, yes, God comes first and then after that, your family is your next ministry. And then you can focus on the "ministry". When you operate with these principles and hold these values it leaves little room for disorder and confusion. Beloved, God is a God of order and if God's ways don't yield positive results then we get to blame Heaven. Which will never happen. So let's do it's God's way and stay loyal to His process and principles and let Him be the one in control.

You do not lose control in a relationship, you reap what your control produces. I think it's smarter to let God have the reins.

You choose.

What the Earthly Marriage Symbolizes

Isaiah 54:5: *For your Maker is your husband, the LORD of hosts is his name; and the Holy One of Israel is your Redeemer, the God of the whole earth he is called.*

Ephesians 5:23,24,32 *For the husband is the head of the wife even as Christ is the head of the church, his body, and is himself its Savior. Now as the church submits to Christ, so also wives should submit in everything to their husbands. This mystery is profound, and I am saying that it refers to Christ and the church.*

From the earliest days of the Christian faith, Christians have honored **holy matrimony** (as Christian marriages are referred to) as a divinely blessed, lifelong, monogamous union between a man and a woman.

The earliest use of the English word "marriage" dates back to the 13th century. Marriage by God's design is the union of one man and one woman (Genesis 2:18). Some say that it is the ceremony (wedding) that makes the man and woman married; however, God's word tells us that it is the joining of flesh that makes the marriage (Genesis 2:24).

The Hebrew word in the Bible is not the English word "marriage". In Hebrew it is called: **kiddushin (sanctification).** Kiddushin is far more binding than an engagement as we understand the term in modern English. Once kiddushin is complete the women is legally the wife of the man. The relationship created by kiddushin can only be dissolved by death or divorce.

God's plan for this relationship is a lifetime relationship of loyalty between a man and a woman that lasts forever.

Hosea 2:19
And I will betroth you to me forever. I will betroth you to me in righteousness and in justice, in steadfast love and in mercy.

Now let's talk about God's plan for marriage. They say that the greatest transaction that you will ever make in your life will be your house. But I beg to differ. I believe that the greatest transaction or contract that you will ever agree too will be that of marriage. Coming into covenant with your spouse is the single most important and greatest transaction and/or decision that you will ever make.

We talked about the importance of real and genuine love in our romantic relationships. But the Bible underscores the value of friendship in your marriage as well:
"Two are better than one, because they have a good return for their work: If one falls down, his friend can help him up. But pity the man who falls and has no one to help him up! Also, if two lie down together, they will keep warm. But how can one keep warm alone? Though one may be overpowered, two can defend themselves"

(Ecclesiastes 4:9-12a).

Naturally, this is one of the reasons that God has created marriage: so that we could have a lifelong friend to help us. But we sometimes underestimate the benefits that God can bring to us and to our marriage through friendship and other friends as well. Remember, Philia love is a threshold of love that must be obtained before we can ever arrive at the level of Agape love. Many marriages would be saved if someone would've reminded them that, "Hey, remember that you guys are best friends".

That's why dating is so important. We develop the friendship in the dating part of the relationship, not in the pic clicking part of the relationship. The courting or dating portion of the relationship has become this terrain to navigate. And love is this glorified, semi-unrealistic thing we fall into by accident now a days. We're supposed to weed out people that aren't compatible and not looking for the same things, and somehow in all that mess, we're supposed to find 'the one.' This lover who will complete us, melt into our lives in all the right ways.

But love isn't like that. **There isn't this magical man or woman who will complete us,** whose heart will fully interweave with ours without conflict or doubt. We don't just find this person and *there is no perfect person, just as we are not perfect.*

People are flawed and difficult. Even in the most wonderful person, there will be ways that he or she doesn't measure up. Our relationships will still be challenging, frustrating, and downright hard. So we can't expect this ideal because it will pull us away, keep us wishing for something we'll never find. Make sure they check the friendship bracket before you start evaluating them for the romantic bracket. Great friends are to be kept for a lifetime.

According to Aristotle, there are three types of friendships: those based on utility, those based on pleasure or delight, and those grounded in virtue. Your spouse or candidate for spouse should check all three of these blocks.

Notwithstanding just the romantic type of friendships, if you keep one or two good friends in your pocket you will be wiser and live a higher quality of life than everyone else that doesn't have any real friends. A person that has one or more really good friends is richer than a person that has a million dollars and no friends. Two things that a person gain in their life with friends are:

1) Learning from Our Friends' Life Experiences

"What has been will be again, what has been done will be done again," we read in **Ecclesiastes 1:9,** *"there is nothing new under the sun."*

And it's better to learn from another person's experience than to have to experience everything ourselves. That's wisdom.

Yet we tend to forget this when facing challenges as a couple, or as individuals. Friendships with other married people are important for this reason.

We need to be able to have straight up conversations about the things that God is teaching us about being a godly husband or wife.

At times this means that we simply share our success or failure stories with true friends, the people we trust.

2) Friends Tell a Truth That No one Else Does

"Faithful are the wounds of a friend, but an enemy multiplies kisses"
(Proverbs 27:6).

The overall meaning of this verse is fairly clear: those who love us truly will tell us the difficult things, while others will gloss over such things and flatter us instead.

Naturally, our spouses often do tell us the difficult things whether we want to hear them to or not. But other friends, proven and loyal friends, can also be a great aid in giving us "faithful wounds", especially in regards to our marriages.

3) Confidence In Someone Outside of Yourself

Proverbs 17:17 ESV
A friend loves at all times,
and a brother is born for adversity

Besides the love of a father, mother, young child or spouse, You will never have a more loyal relationship than that of a friend. So make sure that your spouse is first your friend beloved. Because a friend loveth at all times. I know people that have done jail bids for their friends because they were that loyal to their relationship and friendship. All of Jesus disciples, were loyal unto death, except for Judas, because they were loyal to Jesus. They were committed to the vision and nothing would make them break their word and promises that they made to God through His Son, Jesus Christ. True love is committed beloved. Likewise, Jesus did the same for them and us, by going all of the way to the cross, being crucified, and rising again.

God created us because He's a lover and the lover of our soul. We are His bride, He is the bridegroom and He takes our relationship seriously. In the same way we're supposed to take our earthly marriage vows seriously.

And the characteristics of a Godly marriage are many and I will list a few to end out this chapter, but they are all encompassed in one word, love. **A Godly marriage is one that exemplifies Christ. Remember, God created, instituted, and officiated the first marriage.**

Genesis 1:27-28 ~ *So God created man in his own image, in the image of God he created him; male and female he created them. And God blessed them. And God said to them, "Be fruitful and multiply and fill the earth and subdue it and have dominion over the fish of the sea and over the birds of the heavens and over every living thing that moves on the earth."*

Submit to each other

The man's response in regards to a woman's submission: "A man doesn't own his marriage; he is only the steward of his wife's love." ~ Edwin Louis Cole (Ed Cole)
Mutual submission is a must, however in God's plans and hierarchy there is always order. Marriage is no exception and as a matter of fact is the prototype of God's design.

Isaiah 54:5: *For your Maker is your husband, the LORD of hosts is his name; and the Holy One of Israel is your Redeemer, the God of the whole earth he is called.*

Ephesians 5:23,24,32: *For the husband is the head of the wife even as Christ is the head of the church, his body, and is himself its Savior. Now as the church submits to Christ, so also wives should submit in everything to their husbands. This mystery is profound, and I am saying that it refers to Christ and the church.*

Revelation 19:7-9: *Let us rejoice and exult and give him the glory, for the marriage of the Lamb has come, and his Bride has made* *herself ready; it was granted her to clothe herself with fine linen, bright and pure"— for the fine linen is the righteous deeds of the saints. And the angel said to me, "Write this: Blessed are those who are invited to the marriage supper of the Lamb." And he said to me, "These are the true words of God."*

Celebrate each other

Love gives, Lust takes. The way to differentiate between a person that might be in love and the one who doesn't is the ability of the other to celebrate the other. To push the other and make the mate look good. We live in a society where too many people are killing their relationships with their mouths. How can you say that you love your wife or husband as yourself but you're constantly complaining about them? The answer is you can't.

Protect your spouse. Reaffirm your spouse. It will pay you dividends. You got to love like no one's heart has been broken, sing like no one is listening and dance like no one is watching!

Kill selfishness.

Some of the things that we go through in our relationships are due to selfishness.

- People cheat because they're selfish – They don't really care about what it will do their spouse, their children, and ultimately their whole family and legacy.
- Arguments, especially in front of children are due to selfishness. Never do this because the seed of resentment will be emplaced into your children that will be carried on into their future relationships.

Being loyal is a choice. People will test your relationship. Your ex's will try to find their way back to you because they see you're having great time with your partner. As soon as you start flexing with your boo, I guarantee you that this is when they're going to try to find a way to diminish you, your person, and everything good that is going on in your life. Why? Because love is the greatest flex and if you're doing well then that means that maybe the problem was them and not you. And of course they don't want that beloved.

When you're flexing in the full zenith of your love, rest assured that someone is going to approach your partner as well to test their love and supposed loyalty. And even some of your friends will start to become jealous of your relationship and tell you that you're not good for each other or even tell you bad things about your person. However, it doesn't mean that you have to listen to them. If words is all that it takes to get you to leave the man or woman that God has covenanted you too, your relationship is doomed. Because not everyone is going to be a fan of all of the good things that are going on in your life.

If you are really and truly in a genuine relationship where the foundation is love, be loyal beloved. And if you can't stay loyal to your partner, at least have the decency to breakup with them first, before you commit this type of sin.

Insulate/Protect Your Marriage

A major cause of dissension in marriages is **another opinion** being added to the fray.

Genesis 2:24
English Standard Version (ESV)
24 Therefore a man shall leave his father and his mother and hold fast to his wife, and they shall become one flesh.
Never allow your "friend" to become your confidant whereas you're telling that person things that you won't even tell your spouse.

This breeds insecurity and diminishes the importance of the other individual. Also, God is a God of order. And this is not God's plan or order of things. When you allow outside opinions into your marriage it can change, add, or delete perspectives which is. Component of vision. This is why when you have two visions you have DI-vision. Division leads to confusion and ultimately death.

Finally, the best place in the world is in the arms of someone who will not only hold you at your best, but will pick you up and hug you tight at your weakest moment.

Discern Minor Trouble from Major Trouble

Unfortunately, many marriages end today over troubles that could have been overcome. University of Texas researcher Norval Glenn has found that divorces today are often blamed on problems such as "lack of commitment," "too much conflict and arguing," "unrealistic expectations" and "lack of preparation."

These are problems that both husband and wife can and should work to overcome. Despite what friends, family or popular culture might say, these issues are no reason to end a marriage – especially in light of the serious long-term impact of divorce on your children.

In their book, The Case for Marriage, Maggie Gallagher and Linda Waite explain that couples who think their only options are to either divorce or be miserable often find things getting better if they'll just stick it out. In fact, almost eighty percent of husbands and wives who were very unhappy in their marriage but decided to stay together described themselves as very happy just five years later!

Make a commitment to your spouse to come up a little bit higher. Get refocused regarding your vows and commitments and what's really important in life and then step up. The Bible lets us know in **1 Corinthians 13 that love never fails.** So if your relationship is on the rocks it means that you need to start loving each other a little bit more and watch your relationship fall in place.

It has been commonly taught that woman needs love and men need respect. And it's true. However, to my woman, it doesn't mean that men don't need and want love as well. As a Pastor, of course, I do a lot of marriage and relationship counseling. And I've found that there has been a shift in the matric of the traditional husband and wife relationship. The husband used to be individual in the relationship that I had to encourage to do a little bit more, in terms of affection, loving gestures, and simply just being romantic. But now I counsel the woman on these areas more than the men.

The women during my mother's and grandmother's generation didn't have to be told or taught about setting the mood or being romantic. They didn't have to be told to have that special piece of lingerie on tap that was pleasing to their husband. They didn't have to be told to make sure they keep smelling good. Every woman had a Jane Fonda tape back in the day to make sure that they kept their bodily appearance up. I'm laughing and halfway joking about that, but I'm sure you get the point. The women of every other generation besides our current one understood that their men were visual and it was their duty to satisfy the sexual nature of their man. Don't get cold, boring, and corny woman. Whatever you did to attract that wonderful man that you have, allow it to be your duty to continue these things well into the late years of your marriage.

Encouragement for Women

A woman that operates without love is like a rose without smell. Keep your scent pure and sweet women! In God's wisdom He created you to be soft and subtle and beautiful. Therein lies your strength. There is no love like a mother's love. Your beauty has caused men to kill, nations to rise against nations, and angels to leave their rightful inhabitants. The wisdom of the rose is that even though it can be crushed with one hand you'd dare not because of its beauty and scent. The rose was created in a submitted posture but they just make life so much better. Know your worth, utilize **your** gifts and strengths and may the aroma of your actions and words be the scent that Proverbs 31 says will cause others to look at you and say her husband sure is blessed, her family sure is blessed, **she** is certainly blessed. Be a rose, because a virtuous woman is the best kind of woman.

Encouragement for Men

Men, the greatest gift that you can give your family or leave with your family is love. Money is great and necessary but without love, it means nothing men. And your legacy will be as if you did nothing.

1 Corinthians 13:1-3 (NKJV)

¹ Though I speak with the tongues of men and of angels, but have not love, I have become sounding brass or a clanging cymbal. ² And though I have the gift of prophecy, and understand all mysteries and all knowledge, and though I have all faith, so that I could remove mountains, but have not love, I am nothing. ³ And ᶜthough I bestow all my goods to feed the poor, and though I give my body to be burned, but have not love, it profits me nothing.

Men are to be the protector, provider, and the priest of his home. You are to have the heart of a warrior and a soul of high honor. You are the heartbeat of the home and as you go so does the home. But stay humble. To who much is given, much is required. Too many men let the job title and job description go to their head and then the fabric of their leadership turns into anything but the spirit of love. You are not in a power struggle with your wives or your children because God have instructed them to follow you as you follow Christ. So keep on chasing after Jesus. Live, love, learn, and leave a legacy that brings God glory. If you do this, or if you are doing this, God calls you successful.

DR. LARRY BIRCHETT, JR.

The Dimensions of Love

Love is one of the few things in existence that can traverse through multiple dimensions.
Apostle Dr. Larry Birchett, Jr.

Ephesians 3:17-19 (NKJV)

[17]That Christ may dwell in your hearts through faith; that you, being rooted and grounded in love, [18]may be able to comprehend with all the saints what is the width and length and depth and height— [19]to know the love of Christ which passes knowledge; that you may be filled with all the fullness of God.

We now come to the actual petition which was offered by the Apostle Paul for the church of Ephesus. He was saying that since they have been rooted and grounded in love, they should be able to fully comprehend with all the saints *"what is the breadth, and the length, and the depth, and the height, and to know the love of Christ, which passeth knowledge"*. I want to remind you that we are dealing, not with our love to Him, but with His love to us. God is love and I've been very general in this body of work up to now. But I now want to proceed in a more detailed manner. Before we examine the nature or the character of that knowledge we must consider the knowledge itself, and find out what can be known of the love of God. Apostle Paul sets this before us in an extraordinary manner in the scriptures that I just quoted.

Einstein's 1915 general theory of relativity holds that what we perceive as the force of gravity arises from the curvature of space and time. The scientist proposed that objects such as the Sun and the Earth change this geometry because of their vastness, weight, etc.. And not to get too deep with it, Einstein's theory of relativity has given rise to much discussion of the fourth dimension. It is a twentieth century scientific and mathematical discovery.

But, truth be told, the fourth dimension is nothing new in Biblical or theological thought. The things that we as humans learn is not new knowledge to God. God is Omniscient, to mean that He's all knowing. Everything that mankind learns is already known by God. All of the laws have already been set and as we learn them it becomes what we call, revelation. In short, the fourth dimension is nothing new in Biblical or theological thought. It is as old as God.

Adam fell from information to revelation. When Adam walked with God in the beginning he didn't need revelation. God told him everything. Which is why I always preach that information is better than revelation, because if someone tells you something, it has already been revealed. You don't need any supernatural occurrence or spiritual gift if you already know a thing right? And so, Adam and the rest of mankind since him, besides a few prophets that God has placed in the Earth from now until then, now rely on revelation.

When the Hebrews got mad at Moses in Numbers 12 and started criticizing him, God basically said *are you guys crazy? I speak to Moses face to face!* Meaning that Moses gets his information and directions straight from the source. Moses was higher than any prophet, soothsayer, wise man, or otherwise because he talked directly to God. And in every blessings and privilege that he received, in this same chapter it lets us know that he continued to walk in love and the Bible calls him the most humble and meekest man on Earth. Moses knew about the four dimensions of love before the concept was written about because he knew God and God is love. Moses had relationship. Beloved, there is no love without relationship.

The Apostle Paul wrote about the four dimensions of love in Ephesians chapter 3 verse 18. Watch this:

That Christ may dwell in your hearts by faith; that ye, being rooted and grounded in love, may be able to comprehend with all saints what is the breadth, and length, and depth, and height; And to know the love of Christ, which passeth knowledge, that ye might be filled with all the fullness of God.

Here we see love broken down in four dimensions:

1. Breadth

2. Length

3. Depth

4. Height

These dimensions of love are also wrapped up in **John 3:16**, the most famous verse on Earth,

[16]For God so loved the world that He gave His only begotten Son, that whosoever believeth in Him shall not perish but have everlasting life.

This verse is also sometimes referred to as, "the little gospel" because it contains the whole gospel message in just twenty five words. You see this verse in the end zones of prominent football games, as bumper stickers on the bumpers of cars.

But all of the dimensions from Ephesians 3:18 is there. Let's look at it:

1. Breadth – For God **"so"** loved the world.

God's matchless love is so broad that He includes all men and women of all races, all tribes, all nationalities, all colors, all stations, all levels, of all degrees, of all abilities and attainments. His love is as broad and expansive as humanity. It is unlimited and universal. It is unrestricted by geography, sex, color, rank, or position. It extends over and beyond every human need. It envelops sorrow, loneliness, poverty, disappointment, tragedy, and sin of every kind.

God's love is as broad as human need. It is as boundless as space, as wide as the ocean, and as limitless as the sky.

God's mercy is as wide as the sea. And no matter who you are or what sin you have committed, the first dimension of God's love includes you, hence we get the term breadth.

2. Length – He "gave" His only begotten Son

The second dimension of God's love is length. "He gave." How far did God go? He went to the limit because He gave His only begotten Son. His love went such lengths that it could stop nowhere short of making the supreme gift, the priceless jewel of the heavenly firmament, He gave His only Son. He went all out. He spared nothing. Which is an exteme indication of love. The greatest love is the love where both parties are or are willing to sacrifice something for the other. And in God we see that He provided no cheap sacrifice. His love was long enough to put His Son on the cross to reveal His love to poor, lost, and wretched man.

This is such a wonderful story of love isn't it? Someone reading this book has a been struggling with self-love and self-worth. You feel as though no one could ever love you because somebody has stepped on your self-esteem which has affected your self-worth. Or maybe you have done something that in your mind is so bad that you can't see how anyone, let alone God, can love you. But I want to tell you today, that though you are far away. His love is long enough to reach you, no matter how far away you have wandered. God's love is long enough in sacrifice and long enough in outreach to pull you back. God's love has length. God's love is very long.

3. Depth -- "perish"

The third dimension of God's love is depth -- "might not perish." His love reaches to the very brink of hell. It is deep enough to snatch you from the burning. And God's love can penetrate your heart deep enough to remove the stain and blackness of sin.

It is as deep as the ocean, more penetrating than sin, and more fathomless than the sea. I recall the words of the beautiful song, **"Love Lifted Me"**.

I was sinking deep in sin,

Far from the peaceful shore,

Very deeply stained within,

Sinking to rise no more.

But the Master of the sea

Heard my despairing cry,

From the waters lifted me;

Now safe am I.

Love lifted me, love lifted me;

When nothing else could help,

Love lifted me.

4. Height -- "everlasting life"

The fourth dimension of God's love is height, "everlasting life." His love reaches to the depths to carry us to the heights. He will lift you above the morasses of sin, the fogs of life, the trials of living, the sorrows of earth, up to the heights of His holiness and goodness, where one may live above sin, sorrow, and pain in the celestial ozone of God's eternal city. His topless love will enable you to dwell in heavenly fields and on mountain peaks of the new Mt. Zion in the city of New Jerusalem on the everlasting day. The height of God's love reminds me of refrain of the song, **"Love Lifted Me"** one more time.

Love lifted me
Love lifted me
When nothing else could help
Love lifted me.

Jeremiah, the old prophet, burst forth with these words which he heard God say: *"Yea, I have loved thee with an everlasting love"*
(Jer. 31: 3).

John, the beloved disciple, caught a glimpse of God's great love and cried out, *"Behold, what manner of love the Father hath bestowed upon us, that we should be called the sons of God"* **(I John 3: 1).**

God's love is four-dimensional. It reaches out, and down, and up, and in. It is as broad as man's need; it is as long as the cost of man's redemption; it is as deep as man's sin, and as high as heaven.

No wonder the poet wrote

The love of God is greater far
Than tongue or pen can ever tell;
It goes beyond the highest star,
And reaches to the lowest hell.
Could we with ink the ocean fill,
And were the skies of parchment made;
Were every stalk on earth a quill,
And every man a scribe by trade;
To write the love of God above
Would drain the ocean dry.
Nor could the scroll contain the whole,
Though stretched from sky to sky.

Such matchless, boundless, limitless love of God demands a wholehearted, complete, unreserved response from man.

A husband was in a counselor's office complaining about his wife. "Doesn't your wife keep the house neat?" the marriage counselor asked the husband. "Yes," he replied. "She cooks my favorite dishes and keeps the house spotless."

"Is she kind and generous?" "Yes," replied the husband. "She has a good job, buys me expensive gifts, and is generous to everyone." "Then what is your complaint?"
"She doesn't love me. She's not faithful to me."

And this story is more common than you think. It happens so often. Love is a dimensional force that money and gifts alone cannot equate to. Many elderly parents receive money and gifts from a child, but not loving visits. Many parents in this generation are more worried about what they put on their children instead of what they instill in their children. Basically, what I'm saying is that people decide what they think others should enjoy instead of finding out what they really want. If you cared about what people really wanted you would spend the time to find out exactly what that is.

And we treat God the same way. We think that He should appreciate whatever we decide to give Him: an occasional visit to church, a decent life, a little (or a lot) of money, a mechanical observance of some religious practices.

But the truth is that God wants your love and devotion. God hates formalism and hypocrisy:

I hate, I despise your religious feasts,: I cannot stand your assemblies...".

Amos 5:21

What does the Lord your God ask of you but to fear the Lord your God, to walk in all His ways, to LOVE Him, to serve the Lord your God with all your heart....

Deuteronomy 10:12

So, God hates fake people. Are we clear on that? The Bible teaches us that because of sin, we are estranged from God. Why? Because we have not been faithful to Him. Isaiah says in **Isaiah 59:2** *Your iniquities have separated you from your God.*

But praise God that this particular scripture is not the end of the story. To bring about reconciliation, God sent His own Son to die for our sin and faithlessness and bring us back to Himself:

All this is from God, who reconciled us to himself through Christ.

God made Him who had no sin to be sin for us, so that in Him we might become the righteousness of God.

2 Corinthians 5:18;21

What I'm trying to say is that you should give your heart to God beloved. Don't give him mere tokens, in the form of money or some other cheap token of love. God wants the true and authentic love that He created you for. Don't try to tell God what scraps of your life you will give Him either. Just accept His way of Salvation by faith in Jesus Christ. I guarantee you that ultimately it's the way of joy and peace; now and forevermore.

The Bible shows us the breadth, length, depth, and height in multiple stories. Let's look at one in the book of **Ruth, chapter 3,** and I'm going to skip around in the chapter.

1 Then Naomi her mother-in-law said to her, "My daughter, shall I not seek security for you, that it may be well with you?
2 "Now is not Boaz our kinsman, with whose maids you were? Behold, he winnows barley at the threshing floor tonight.
3 "Wash yourself therefore, and anoint yourself and put on your best clothes, and go down to the threshing floor; but do not make yourself known to the man until he has finished eating and drinking.
4 "It shall be when he lies down, that you shall notice the place where he lies, and you shall go and uncover his feet and lie down; then he will tell you what you shall do."
5 She said to her, "All that you say I will do."
BOAZ SAID: 9 He said, "Who are you?" And she answered, "I am

Ruth your maid. So spread your covering over your maid, for you are a close relative."
10 Then he said, "May you be blessed of the LORD, my daughter. You have shown your last kindness to be better than the first by not going after young men, whether poor or rich.
11 "Now, my daughter, do not fear. I will do for you whatever you ask, for all my people in the city know that you are a woman of excellence.
12"Now it is true I am a close relative; YET, there is a relative closer than I."

Boaz and Ruth is probably the best love story in the Bible, not because of the 'romance' quotient in it but because their relationship has God pouring out of its fibers. To all of my singles who are confused, anxious and a little bit troubled about your future life partner, You can stand to learn great lessons from the book of Ruth.

Naomi sends Ruth in the night to go to Boaz and asked her to lie at his feet. Ruth replied obediently *"All that you say I will do."* She never asked, 'how can I be sure he is the guy?' or even something like *'this plan seems weird'* even thought it was. She just unconditionally obeyed the woman from whom she heard and learned about the one and true Jehovah God. We need to all learn a lesson from Ruth and learn to respect the wisdom of the Godly men and women that God has strategically placed in our lives.

It doesn't matter what the person has done in error in the past if God still has His hands on them we should respect and even revere certain words of advice and instruction that comes from them because what they're saying is coming from God Himself. At the point of their giving us guidance they are literally the ambassador of God on Earth for us.

When I think about this thought, I'm always reminded how David still respected and even revered Saul and Saul's ordained position because David knew that God put him there. And we all know that God had already rejected Saul and that Saul was terrible to David even to the point of trying to kill him multiple times, but for David, disrespecting the man that God still had in place was not an option. And ultimately God honored David because God honors honor.

Don't lose your blessing because of your feelings beloved. Learn to love what God loves and abhor what God abhors. God is not random or messy. If He has something in place it's on purpose for a purpose and not accidental or an oversight on God's behalf. Remember that.

Listen, when the motive of your action is obedience and fulfilling the will of God, then God will never allow you to go in the wrong direction, but if you have already decided to go your way then the result is chaos.

Boaz was shocked to see Ruth inside his bed room; however, his actions and words are priceless, he does not take advantage of the situation, he gently told her " Yes, I am your close relative and I have rights to redeem you, yet, there is another man who is closer than me, so I need to check with him before I go ahead in this matter. Isn't he a man of impeccable character? Boaz was middle aged, while Ruth though a widow was young. He knew her good character and hard work, yet instead of grabbing her to be his wife, he patiently waits for God to clear the way. Wow this is amazing! I can hear Boaz telling Ruth, 'Well let's do it the right way, according to the custom and rules of this society.'

Psalm 37:23
"The steps of a good man are ordered by the Lord: and he delighteth in his way."

The practical application that applies to our daily life is that we cannot do whatever seems right in our eyes. Are you listening? **Rules have to be followed**, the Bible says:

Deuteronomy 12:8 *"You shall not do at all what we are doing here today, every man doing whatever is right in his own eyes."*

Proverbs 21:2 *"Every way of man is right in his own eyes, but the Lord weighs the hearts.".*

Driving the car with a license, using the computer with software purchased rather than pirated software, doing business with the proper Government permit, constructing houses or churches with proper government approvals are all essential factors to be followed by EVERY Christian. **We have to do it right**, without skipping any rules. Are you listening?

The aforementioned are all natural things, but we have spiritual principles to follow too: not shacking up before marriage, not cussing, no lying, no stealing, paying your tithes off of everything that God gives us, praying without ceasing, being anxious for nothing, walking by faith and not by sight! Get the point?

B) Let me give you another example from the Bible

King Saul: **1 Samuel 13:5** *Now the Philistines assembled to fight with Israel, 30,000 chariots and 6,000 horsemen, and people like the sand which is on the seashore in abundance; and they came up and camped in Michmash, east of Beth-aven.*
6 When the men of Israel saw that they were in a strait (for the people were hard-pressed), then the people hid themselves in caves, in thickets, in cliffs, in cellars, and in pits.
7 Also some of the Hebrews crossed the Jordan into the land of Gad and Gilead. But as for Saul, he was still in Gilgal, and all the people followed him trembling.

8 Now he waited seven days, according to the appointed time set by Samuel, but Samuel did not come to Gilgal; and the people were scattering from him.
9 So Saul said, "Bring to me the burnt offering and the peace offerings." And he offered the burnt offering.
10 As soon as he finished offering the burnt offering, behold, Samuel came; and Saul went out to meet him and to greet him.

Listen to me friends , Prophet Samuel had clearly said in **1 Samuel 10:8**: *"Go down ahead of me to Gilgal. I will surely come down to you to sacrifice burnt offerings and fellowship offerings, but you must wait seven days until I come to you and tell you what you are to do."*

To be fair, the circumstances that king Saul was facing was not ideal. They weren't small at all. The Philistines assembled to fight with Israel, 30,000 chariots and 6,000 horsemen, and people like the sand of the seashore was present. People were hiding themselves in caves, in thickets, in cliffs, in cellars, and in pits. Some of the Hebrews crossed the Jordan into the land of Gad and Gilead. But as for Saul, he was still in Gilgal. Let me say it again, (he was still in Gilgal) and all the people followed him trembling. How many of us would have been anywhere except for Gilgal in this situation? But Saul was still there.

And on top of all that, he waited to the seventh day, according to the appointed time set by Samuel, but he just didn't wait long enough. He was supposed to wait until Samuel showed up. Beloved, you can still lose your trial simply by not being patient enough. Delay does not mean denial and just because God is not showing up when you think He should doesn't mean that He's not going to show up. He may not come when you want Him too but He always comes on time.

People were scattering all over the place. It seemed like he was losing control. And He was, just as God wanted him to, because God wants all of the credit. It was his time to exhibit faith. It was his time to wait on the answer. God put him in the waiting room. And when you are in God's waiting room just know that there is a release coming. God is about to release you into your healing. God is about to release you into your next season. God is about to release you into a higher level in Him. You just have to be disciplined enough to see the manifestation of what God already has purposed for you anyway. The fruit of discipline is better than the fruit of regret. So stay disciplined.

It's while you are in His waiting room, spiritual fruit is literally being grown on you and in you. But you have to wait on Him and wait in Him. God was trying to develop the spiritual fruit of Longsuffering and Peace in him. And spiritual fruit grows through experiences. So, if you don't allow God to take you through things you won't ever fully develop.

But everything that was happening around Saul was denting and smashing his faith. He waited for seven days BUT did not have patience to wait until the end of the day and he dared to disobey God and His Word, he offered the burnt offering himself, though he was neither priest nor prophet; yet, as a king, he thought he can do anything, a piece of presumption which another king, King Uzziah paid dearly for and became leprous.

2 Chronicles 26:19: *"But Uzziah, with a censer in his hand for burning incense, was enraged; and while he was enraged with the priests, the leprosy broke out on his forehead before the priests in the house of the LORD, beside the altar of incense."*

Back to Saul. God was very angry with Saul and judgment was passed. Let's go back to 1 Kings 13:

13 Samuel said to Saul, "You have acted foolishly; you have not kept the commandment of the LORD your God, which He commanded you, for now the LORD would have established your kingdom over Israel forever.
14 "But now your kingdom shall not endure. The LORD has sought out for Himself a man after His own heart, and the LORD has appointed him as ruler over His people, because you have not kept what the LORD commanded *you."*

I believed that Samuel was offended. Be careful when you offend the men and women of God. When an ordained man or woman of God is operating under divine instructions from God Himself, be careful. Because they are at that time, the voice of God Himself on earth. So when you go against a person that is acting in obedience to God's voice you must understand that if you come against them, you're coming against God Himself.

And that's why we shouldn't be worried about enemies. Those that are enemies of us are actually the enemies of God. **That's why I love the scripture Romans 8:31:** *If God be for us, who can be against us.*

We have to live lives that are pleasing to God. We have to live lives that don't bring offense to God in anything.

(2 Corinthians 6:3–4 KJV).
"Giving no offense in anything, that the ministry be not blamed: but in all things approving ourselves as the ministers of God, in much patience, in afflictions, in necessities, in distresses"

Responsibility is always attached to Blessings. Working comes before eating, Love come before marriage, The Hebrews had to cross the wilderness to get to the promise. Repentance comes before Salvation. And God measures success by faithfulness not by worldly success.

If you want something that tastes good and not only look good how many of you know that you cannot skip steps? I really like chocolate chip cookies but I don't want cookies that only look like they're good, I want cookies that is good. I want cookies with the right ingredients in them. You have to have the right amount of eggs, the right amount of milk or water, the right amount of salt, the right amount of flour. The dough has to be just right. I don't only want cookies that look scrumptious, I want cookies that are scrumptious. Cookies that have been baked for the appropriate amount of time, not just put in the oven to brown and then taken out. Get the point? The blessing of enjoying a great chocolate chip cookie can only be enjoyed after certain responsibilities have been taken seriously.

If you want a good marriage, how many of you know that you can't skip any steps? People, find out that me and my wife got married in less than a year and so they always ask me, "Apostle, how long should you wait before you get married?" But every relationship is different, and every relationship requires a different amount of time. My answer to you is **spend the necessary time** to find out if that person is toxic.

- Spend the necessary time to see if that person is kind!
- Spend the necessary time to see if that person can take care of themselves (physically, mentally, spiritually, and financially)!
- Spend the necessary time to find out if that person is faithful!
- Spend the necessary time to find out if that person is loving!
- Spend the necessary time to find out if the person brings peace to your life or division!

You have to spend the necessary time to see if this person is your person because the worst prison in the world is a home without peace. So be careful with who you fall in love with or marry beloved. The time that it took for me and my wife to determine that we were destined to be together forever might be different for another couple and likewise, the necessary time to figure this out will differ as well. At one point in my life, I was busy trying to choose my life and in the end it didn't work out. This time, God chose my wife and we're heading happily to twenty years of love and marriage. I learned to not be led by emotions and I learned to be disciplined. The lesson of discipline is better than the lesson of regret.

And let me go back to the money. Just because a person has money when you meet them doesn't mean that they know how to make money or has always had money.

Making money is an action. But keeping money is a behavior. And on top of all of that, growing money is wisdom. Spend the necessary time to find out if this person has the right actions, behaviors, and wisdom when it comes to the subject of money. I mean that.

Practical applications in our life:

1) When we receive a word from the Lord, we need to wait till the end, I would add to this and say, 'wait even after that' until we get a sure assurance from the Lord. **Don't jump to conclusions,** let the Word of God be you only reference and nothing else.

2) Whatever we do, we need to do it the right way and God's way, then we will have 100 % success.

My personal testimony is that during covid everybody was pressuring us to get the free ppl loans and all of this stuff. They were telling us to not come to the church, to not pay the mortgage and all of that.

We didn't take any fake free money, (because it wasn't free). We didn't stop paying anything (because when it was over people were getting kicked out of their properties because they had 30 days to pay everything). We still came to church and hence we're still here. You have to be able to endure the process men and women of God. Good things come to them that wait. God has never been late! He's never early and he's never late, He's just right on time.

Basically what I'm trying to tell you beloved is to not skip the process. Before God allows you to realize your dream or His purpose for your Ife He will always test your character. Let God prove you. Let God test you and when you come through with flying colors, He will promote you to your next season.

The Apostle Paul reached one of the greatest peaks in all of his inspired writings when he attempted to describe the four-dimensional love of God. *That Christ may dwell in your hearts by faith; that ye, being rooted and grounded in love, May be able to comprehend with all saints what is the breadth, and length, and depth, and height; And to know the love of Christ, which passeth knowledge, that ye might be filled with all the fullness of God.*

Ephesians 3:18 (MSG); 20 NKJV

[18]*My response is to get down on my knees before the Father, this magnificent Father who parcels out all heaven and earth. I ask him to strengthen you by his Spirit—not a brute strength but a glorious inner strength—that Christ will live in you as you open the door and invite him in. And I ask him that with both feet planted firmly on love, you'll be able to take in with all followers of Jesus the extravagant dimensions of Christ's love. Reach out and experience the breadth! Test its length! Plumb the depths! Rise to the heights! Live full lives, full in the fullness of God.*

[20]*Now unto him that is able to do exceeding abundantly above all that we ask or think, according to the power that worketh in us,*

Unto him be glory in the church by Christ Jesus throughout all ages, world without end. Amen.

May the Force Be With You

Being deeply loved by someone gives you strength, while loving
someone deeply gives you courage.

Apostle Dr. Larry Birchett, Jr.

Proverbs 17:17 (NKJV)

A friend loves at all times, and a brother is born for adversity.

The Bible tells us in John 1, that God is love and then in Romans 5
it explains that He (God) commended His love toward us in that
while we were yet sinners Christ died for us. And then in 1 John it
says *beloved, let us love one another for love is of God and everyone
that loveth is born of God and knoweth God. He that loveth not,
loveth not God for God is love.* The translation of the flow of
scripture that I just presented is that **I was fashioned in love by love
to love and be loved.**

1 John 4:16-21 (NIV)
[16] *And so we know and rely on the love God has for us. God is
love. Whoever lives in love lives in God, and God in him.*
[17] *In this way, love is made complete among us so that we will have
confidence on the day of judgment, because in this world we are
like him.*
[18] *There is no fear in love. But perfect love drives out fear, because
fear has to do with punishment. The one who fears is not made
perfect in love.*
[19] *We love because he first loved us.*
[20] *If anyone says, "I love God," yet hates his brother, he is a liar.
For anyone who does not love his brother, whom he has seen,
cannot love God, whom he has not seen.*

²¹ And he has given us this command: Whoever loves God must also love his brother.

The force that makes the world go round is love. It's the energy, for lack of a better word, and force that caused God to create us in the first place. To not know God is to not know the source of the greatest force in existence. To not have a relationship with God, the source of the greatest force is to resign yourself to a life of inferiority to those who do know and have a relationship with love.

"May the force be with you," is the great slogan from the movie series called Star Wars. The Force, in the movie, is a mysterious energy field created by life that binds the galaxy together. Harnessing the power of "the Force" gives the Jedi and/or the Sith, and others sensitive to this spiritual energy extraordinary abilities. The movie is talking about an ethereal unseen force that a person can tap into to make them extraordinary; physically, mentally, and spiritually. The movie is fictional but the concept is biblical. Because this "Force" that the movie is always mysteriously referring too actually exists, and it's called love.

If you harness the power of love it will enable you to do extraordinary things. The Bible says in 1 Peter 4:8 that *"love covers a multitude of sins."* The force enables you to do that. To cover sin is to forgive it, and forgiveness is associated with love. That's powerful. 1 Corinthians 13 says that love *"is not easily provoked."* That's a superpower beloved, trust me. Simply put, love is one of the most powerful things there is. Love between two lovers, a parent, a child, friends, sisters, brothers. Love sometimes is the only force that can propel us into action for another person.

I remember one time I had to do a wedding in Ohio. Mind you, we were living in Pennsylvania at the time. My wife Joanna, my youngest son Jayden, and I took the trip. We were staying in a very nice hotel the day before leading up to the wedding rehearsal and wedding. My wife, Jayden, and myself went down to the pool to blow off some steam. Our son Jayden was about 5 years old at the time.

My wife and he went in ahead of me because I was talking to someone or something. Long story short, as soon as he and Joanna got into pool area he made his way straight to the pool. He ran and just jumped into the pool. In his mind, he thought he could swim. He could not. I came in on the tail end as he was hitting the water and I saw him struggling in the water going down and coming up and gasping for air with a look of fear on his face. At that moment a force came over me that I've only felt a few times in my life and without thinking I sprinted to the water and just jumped in, not thinking about the clothes that I still had on or the phone that was in my pocket or footwear that was on my feet. My only thought was that I have to save my son.

I praise God for His grace in that situation because I was able to hop in the water in time and pretty easily get him out of the pool. But I'll never forget the moment or the feeling. I felt invincible. All I could think about was the love that I had for my youngest child and he needed my help. It was that love that propelled me to the water and just made me jump in without thinking, even though I'm not that strong of a swimmer myself.

When you are operating from a place of love, so much more than normal is possible. It'll make you do things that you never knew you could do. It'll give you the strength to endure under incredible duress and perform feats that you never could've completed without the element of love. You can also let go of unforgiveness, judgment, resentment, fear, and so much more as long as love is present. And that's why it says in 1 Corinthians 13, *"love never fails."*

I believe that love can start and finish wars. Over the last few years we have seen an influx of police brutality against helpless civilians. And in some cases these instances seem to have been fueled by bias and a spirit of racism. I am commonly asked by local leaders and parishioners of my thoughts on the Black Lives Matter protests and other demonstrations and marches that are being enacted all over the United States of America. And my response is that it's a sin issue, not a skin issue. It comes down to egregious abuse of power and ego, all underlined by a feeling of superiority over anyone else that's not in law enforcement for those officers involved.

Bias, discrimination, and racism are sins motivated by pride. And I'm referring to the worse kind of pride, luciferian pride. satan didn't get kicked out of Heaven because he wanted to be God, he got kicked out of Heaven because he wanted to be like God. Many law enforcement officers, regardless of race, have a God complex. They think that they are the beginning and ending of anything that pertains to law and lawbreaking. Because they feel this way any other interpretation of what they have perceived as error, in any given situation will not be received favorably by them. Of course this leads to provocation and the provoking element is always fueled by pride.

When pride is present any kind of disagreement will provoke the one that is infected. Why? Because this kind of person feels superior. This kind of person feels entitled. This kind of person sees themselves as god.

Hate can't defeat this kind of spirit only love can. You cannot defeat love with hate, only love can do this. **Love is the greatest protest beloved.** It's okay to protest, but you have to do it the right way. Stop looting, burning, and tearing up your own neighborhoods. Stop fighting fire with fire and start using the water of the Holy Spirit to allow love to rain on the situation.

Darkness cannot drive out darkness; only light can do that. Hate cannot **drive out hate**; only **love can** do that."

Martin Luther King, Jr.

In everything we do we must remember that God is looking at our hearts. If you're marching and protesting in anger, the fruit of your actions will be the result of anger. Somebody probably is going to get killed or hurt or incarcerated. However, if you're marching and demonstrating in love, you will get the fruit of love.

"The fruit of the Spirit is love, joy, peace, patience, kindness, generosity, faithfulness, gentleness, self-control..."

Galatians 5:22-23

Love Is the Supreme Christian Virtue. "The greatest of these is love," Paul says. No wonder, then, that it's mentioned first on the list of the fruit of the Spirit: "But the fruit of the Spirit is love." We see here that *Fruit* is singular. It's not the *fruits* of the Spirit, but the *fruit*. The fruit is a unit, and that unity may be called Christlike character. One thing that we have to remember is that unity does not always mean uniformity. Just because we're on the same team, so to speak, or in the same family or faith, means that we're all going to look the same, dress the same, sound the same, or act the same. Unity does not mean uniformity. Allow for freedom of expression which is the dignity of the gift of existence.

But it's not the Spirit-inspired writing of Paul that will instruct us, but that of the Apostle John, otherwise known as the *beloved disciple* or the *Apostle of Love*. John is called the Apostle of Love because of the prominence of the theme in his first letter, known as First John.

Beloved, let us love one another, for love is from God, and whoever loves has been born of God and knows God. Anyone who does not love does not know God, because God is love. In this the love of God was made manifest among us, that God sent his only Son into the world, so that we might live through him. In this is love, not that we have loved God but that he loved us and sent his Son to be the propitiation for our sins. Beloved, if God so loved us, we also ought to love one another. No one has ever seen God; if we love one another, God abides in us and his love is perfected in us.
1 John 4:7-12

But again the million dollar question is what is love? And how should we define biblical "agape" love? Here is a definition as it pertains to it being the fruit: **Love is the consistent demonstration**

of putting others before yourself. It is unconditional and self-sacrificial for the healthy empowerment of another. It is the outworking of the life of God within you.

Love is being open to experiencing the other person exactly for who they are and loving all of them. When you come from that place, you are harnessing the power of love. You have to be able to love yourself, flaws and all and likewise because loving anyone outside of yourself is a choice when it comes to romantic and relational love, you will have to choose to love that person's fruit and flaws as well. Because a flawless person doesn't exist and to purport to be flawless or to love a perfect person would be and is disingenuous. Or to put it as the younger generation would put, you're being fake.

That's why you have to grow through what you go through! Fruit are the things that grow over time. Spiritual fruit is grown in us through experiences.

NBC News ran a story on April 29, 2023 about a Paralympic athlete that stopped during the London Marathon to help a runner who collapsed. While running the London Marathon, **Richard Whitehead**, an athlete who has competed in the Paralympics, stopped to help a runner who collapsed. I want to stop right here in the recollection of this story to point out that this kind of gesture came from somewhere. This was fruit on exhibit. This was love in action and we need to understand that this kind gesture came from somewhere deep within the paralympic runner's soul.

First of all, Richard Whitehead, the paralympic runner was competing too. And of course he had to know that stopping to help someone else would hurt his time. But when they interviewed him afterward, he said that we have to understand is that it's not just about when you pass the finish line, it's about how you pass the finish line! I was floored when I heard him say that. But his fruit was clearly showing. He has grown through what he's been through.

This man has been through too many real life experiences to not understand and know that there are things that are way more important than the race. And his sensitivity or awareness of this fact came from somewhere. Maybe the process of enduring the loss of his legs or something else but his fruit was showing in his thought process and what he deemed to be more important at that time.

That type of thinking. That type of mindset, that there are things that are more important than winning a race, we call that fruit and a person that has excellent character. Mr. Whitehead didn't allow the circumstances of his life to make him bitter, he became better. Don't get bitter, get better beloved.

It's the same thing that Peter did to the lame man laying at the gate called Beautiful in Acts 3. The lame man was begging for money but Peter and John realized instantly that he needed something way more important than alms.

Acts 3:6 (KJV)

Then Peter said, Silver and gold have I none; but such as I have I give thee: In the name of Jesus Christ of Nazareth rise up and walk.

The Holy Spirit is saying to somebody reading this book right now to stop belly aching and get up and walk. Stop making excuses and rise up and walk. Stop blaming your mommy and your daddy and your aunty and your uncle and rise up and walk. We all know that you have a testimony but get your butt up, brush yourself up and walk. It's time beloved!

I mean Richard Whitehead, could've chosen to take the bitter road. He could've said, 'I'm a double amputee, I'm out here running with prosthetics, life has not been easy for me!' 'This guy got two good legs, life has been so good to him! I am not helping him or nobody, I'm just going to think about myself.' But he didn't.

He has done the work and more importantly somebody has done the work in him. That somebody is the Holy Spirit. And we call that type of thinking and acting the work of the Holy Spirit.

Only the Holy Spirit can cause you to help others when they are down, even when it doesn't benefit you. That's what you call charity. That's what you call love.

The measure of a man is not measured by what he does for people that can help him, it is determined by how that man treats the person that can't do anything for him.

Thomas Aquinas, an Italian Dominican friar and priest, an influential philosopher, and theologian, from the 13th century, pointed out that numbered among the attributes of the Fruit of the Holy Spirit are certain virtues, such as charity, meekness, faith, chastity, and kindness. Augustine of Hippo, a theologian and philosopher who was also the Bishop of Hippo Regius in Numidia, Roman North Africa, defined virtue as "a good habit consonant with our nature."

The *Catechism of the Catholic Church,* and of course I'm not Catholic and this is not a Catholic book but I think this information is noteworthy, defines this fruit as "perfections that the Holy Spirit forms in us as the first fruits of eternal glory" (CCC 1832). Basically, if we are living a "life of the Spirit," these "fruits" will be found in our lives.

Most translations of the above passage only list nine fruits, while the Latin Vulgate provides a list of 12 fruits, adding **modesty, generosity, and chastity.**

But the fruit of the Spirit is, charity, joy, peace, patience, benignity, goodness, longanimity, mildness, faith, modesty, continency, chastity. Against such there is no law
(Galatians 5:22-23 Douay-Rheims).
Just remember that whether you go with nine fruits or twelve fruits or one-hundred fruits, they all boil down to one, love. And the fruit of love will keep you from sinning against God, yourself, and other people. The fruit destroys the root of sin in your life.

One of the most common goodbye greetings is "May God be with you". Or "May God go with you". This is one of the greatest blessings that you can give to a person because you are actually saying, "May the force of love be with you". It's a powerful blessing.

As **1 John 4:16** states, *Whoever lives in love, lives in God and God in him.* So to tell a person, "May God go with you" is right in line with God's Word and it is what we call in church language, good doctrine.

In Star Wars, Luke Skywalker was the star of the whole movie series that would one day be so strong with the "force" that he'd bring the evil empire down. And eventually, he did. In the Bible, Jesus Christ of Nazareth, born in Bethlehem, was the person that would one day be so full of the "force" of love, that he'd one day use it to tear satan's kingdom down. And He did that on the cross.

And so I say to you beloved, let the force be with you. Because it is the way. Love is the way and it will defeat anything that tries to quench it.

As a Pastor, obviously I do a lot of counseling to include pre-marital and marital counseling. When I am discussing relationships of course the subject of love comes up. Especially with pre-marital counseling clients or actual members. And I kind of let them speak a little bit about love and what they think or feel love actually is. And I normally ask them regarding how do they know that they're in love. And occasionally someone will say something like, "I fell in love, I just couldn't help it...", and I have to tell them that no, we don't fall in love; we choose to love. And then sometimes I am led to take it further and tell them that they don't really know what love is. And if you don't know what love is, how can you love someone else? Some people cry right then and there when they realize that this, in fact, is true concerning them.

But I'd rather them to find out this truth right there with me in an obscure church office than after spending $15k on a wedding that will end in a little of 5 years or less because they didn't marry for love. They married for the appearance of it. Love is the greatest flex beloved, not the appearance of it. People try to fake it all of the time but the truth be told is that if private cameras were utilized to expose even the private moments of these persons lives they're not happy. So don't marry for the sake of having a nice wedding and the appearance of being in love. Marry for love because love is the greatest gift that this life can give us.

To love or be loved is the question? The answer requires a choice to be made on either end. Love is a choice, not something that you fall into, or something that you can experience without your permission. You have to give love permission. You have to give yourself permission to love and be loved by someone else. As I have already taught you in this book, love is a force, a fiery and unstoppable force that you have to open up to so that it can come in. And once you let this divine, Godly force in, it ignites your heart, and like a wildfire it grows and grows until it encompasses your body, mind, and soul.

And this is why you can't buy love, you can't force love, you can't plan love, and you can't predict love. It's an organic thing that comes directly from the Ancient of Days, Jehovah God, Elohim Himself, according to His will and purpose for our lives. It's His most special gift to all of His creation. And the most famous scripture of all time denotes this fact in that **John 3:16** declares that, *"For God so **loved** the world, that He gave His only begotten Son. That whosoever believeth in Him shall not perish but have everlasting life."* He literally demonstrated His love for us in the personage of His Son Jesus Christ. Which is why life without Jesus is like an unsharpened pencil, it has no point.

There is an old saying that says "It's better to have loved and lost than never to have loved before." I've come to believe that this is one of the truest statements ever coined. Because we don't know how long we're going to live. We don't know what God's plan for our lives truly entail to the detail. So, if it's in His plan for you to have a short life, but He allowed love in that short life via parents, siblings, spouse, and children; you are most blessed of all men and/or women that have ever lived. On the other hand, if you have lived a long life yet have never experienced all of the facets of love, your life has been far less blessed than the one who has had a short life with love in it.

So, even though God doesn't owe any of us anything except to love us and take care of us, because He did say that He shall supply all of our needs; keep in mind that He hasn't promised us that we would receive every human blessing and pleasure that this life has to offer. Still, never forget that the gift of life itself is a privilege. The fact that He has blown the breath of life into our bodies is simply amazing and is the very reason that we exist. On top of all of that, if He has allowed love in your life, no matter how short and fleeting it was, then you have lived the most amazingly successful life already. That's right successful. A Successful life is one where God gets the glory. And it's always a win-win because when God gets all the Glory because He's pleased and then you get the benefits. By the way, benefits is not just popularity and money. Benefits can mean long life, a peaceful life, and a life full of love. When I was young we used to sing a song in church with lyrics that sang, "when the praises go up, the blessings come down."

Only what you do for God is going to last. Not the accolades or money or houses and cars. When you get to Heaven, God is not going to ask you how big your bank account was beloved. He's not going to be impressed by the wonderful position that you held while you were on Earth beloved. Success can be additionally gaged by the amount of love that you expressed to and for God and the amount of love that you have experienced in your life. So, change your thinking beloved to that of a heavenly mindset. because you have just learned that you are a huge success in the eyes of God and the economy of Heaven.

"Do not be conformed to this world, but be transformed by the renewing of your mind..."

Romans 12:2, NKJV

Mindset is huge. Whatever you magnify will manifest. Or in other words, your life will move in the direction of your most dominant thoughts. If you're constantly down on yourself thinking you'll never get ahead, then you won't. But if you'll choose to believe that you are an overcomer, that you have victory up ahead, that God has good things in store for your future; then that's what you'll end up with. That's why it's so important to make sure our thoughts are the same as God's thoughts.

Just like a computer, whatever you allow into your mind is what will come out in your attitude, actions, and words. And that's why your words matter beloved. Words are vibrations. Words have many layers and are more than just a way to communicate because words have energy - they hold a vibration, have power, and can sometimes reveal our secrets. I can always discern when a person has a romantic interest in someone that they're trying to discuss casually when they're in my office. And sometimes I'm able to pick up bitterness or anger and sometimes even regret. Our words have a way of telling on us because our word have an energy, a vibration that can be detected. That's the premise behind the science of the Lie Detector.

Every word carries an energy that can be sensed, regardless of whether you're speaking, hearing it, thinking it, or reading it out of a book. There are many elements that comprise and affects a word's energy. Words are the vibration of nature. Good words create good natured things. Ugly words create bad natured things. Remember, God created the world, which the Hebrew word really is translated as Cosmos, with His mouth and He said that what He had created (said) was good. The word universe comes from a Latin root word whereas cosmos comes from a Greek word. What you need to know and understand is that cosmos is the total opposite of chaos. So God created everything in order on order of His words for His purpose.

Words have the power to impact us both negatively and positively on a daily basis, so speak positively every day, speak life every day. Solomon told us in the book of Proverbs that life and death is in the power of your tongue. He was the wisest man that ever lived, besides Jesus, so if I were you, I'd listen to him.

However, it's hard to think good thoughts when you keep inputting bad data in it. You can't be a frequent customer at the bars, strip clubs, and a constant listener of hardcore rock music, gangster rap, and an avid watcher of porn and horror movies and think that you're going to have positive and powerful thoughts. The more you meditate on God's Word, the more you will transform your thinking to be like God's thinking. Choose today to focus on the Word of God. Allow your mind to be renewed. As you focus on God's thoughts, you will become more like Him, the force of love will be with you in a higher measure, and you will see His hand of blessing in every area of your life.

Whatever you do consistently over 21 days becomes a habit. So be consistent in your speech and watch your life line up itself to the energy of your words.

We have established that words are vibrations and that every word carries its own energy. And that's why names are so important, because names identify the nature of the person, place, or thing that has been named. Names are so important that we've seen God change a few names of certain people in the Bible that had unique purposes such as Abram to Abraham, Jacob to Israel, Simon to Peter, Saul to Paul, and many more.

In Old Testament times and even New Testament times we see that babies were given names corelating to their perceived purposes and circumstances of their birth. Such as Jabez, which means sorrowful or borne in pain. Jacob, which means trickster, supplanter, or overreach. Esau meant hairy, and etc. And some were given names based on expectation. Jesus, is one of two people in the Bible whose name or title was given to them before they were born. The name that I'm referring to concerning Jesus is Christ, which means anointed, as in the "anointed one" which comes from the word Messiah. The Greek word Christos translates into the Hebrew word of the same meaning. The other person given his name before his birth was John the Baptist. The angel Gabriel told Zechariah, his father, that his wife Elizabeth, who was barren, would bear a child that would prepare the way for Jesus the Christ, and they were to name him John. John's name means God is gracious.

Since we're on the subject of names and have established that names are important, let me just say that Lucifer is not, was not and never has been the name of satan, nor was he the firstborn angel, nor do angels have a mother. satan isn't a name either, by the way, it's a title, which means resister or adversary. This is important to know especially if you ever expect to be effective in Deliverance, which is the casting out or away of demons from a person that has been afflicted with this type of situation. Not that you talk to demons, but if they ever talk to you while occupying the body of a host, if you can determine their name, you can cast them out easier, of course using the name of Jesus.

Angels are spirit creatures, a higher order of life than man, and were created individually. They were not "born", nor was there any element of sexual reproduction involved. And this is another element of the temptation that caused them to leave their first estate as it is stated in Jude, to come down to Earth and sleep with women, as it is written in Genesis 6. They were lured by the gift of sex that was given only to humans also with the added element of creation, whereas we then get to enjoy the miracle of birth. Before God created Adam and then Eve out of Adam and commanded them to be fruitful and multiply, the angels had no concept of reproduction in the way that we're able to do it. Refer to Genesis 6 to read about how certain angels left Heaven to come to Earth to sleep with our women and produced giants on the Earth, the race of Nephiliim. Adam was given the task and authority to name all of the animals, birds, creeping things on the Earth, and things in the sea. Adam was also given the privilege to name Eve and what's important about these things is that anything that you name you have dominion over.

Lucifer, incidentally, is a Latin word. Latin as a language is literally thousands of years younger than Hebrew. Lucifer is a mistranslation of the Hebrew word הֵילֵל, which means shining one. It is not a proper name. Jerome, who translated the Bible from the Hebrew into Latin, didn't recognize this and thought it was a name, and so substituted הֵילֵל, helel, with Lucifer, old Latin for Venus, the morning star.

A whole corpus of nonsense has sprung up from that mistake. Seriously, ask yourself, why would the Devil's name as an angel be Latin?

Incidentally, the only occurrence of "Lucifer" in some translations of the Bible actually refers to the King of Babylon, an ancient Mesopotamian city from which grew an Empire; the king in question was almost certainly Nebuchadnezzar II, a contemporary of the prophet Daniel, who sacked Jerusalem and took the Jews into exile. (Isaiah 14:4)

Now, I thought it was important to take the time to give you that information because we're talking about using the force, specifically the force of love. And it was the love of Jesus that compelled Him to send the Holy Spirit to be with us so that greater works we can do than even He did. Keep in mind that Jesus prayed to the Father to send the Holy Spirit to us.

16And I will pray the Father, and He will give you another Helper, that He may abide with you forever.

John 14:16 (NKJV)

Jesus knew that we would need a force that is stronger than the force of evil that has been loosed on Earth. Because of His love for us, He gave us the Holy Force, which is also known as the Holy Ghost or the Holy Spirit. This force works even better when we identify people, places, and things properly, in the spirit of truth.

17The Spirit of Truth; whom the world cannot receive, because it neither sees Him nor knows Him; but you know Him, for He dwells with you and will be in you.

John 14:17 (NKJV)

Praise God that the Holy Spirit lives within us and gives us the discernment necessary to overcome all of the tricks of the enemy. If we're not operating with the Holy Spirit we're operating in self, lies, and deception. And that's why the prophet Hosea taught us that many people perish for lack of knowledge. So stop trying to cast out satan out of every demonically touched individual, most likely it's not him in them.

Likewise, it's through the names of God that the nature of God is revealed to us. Who is God in His fullness? How has He expressed His riches and righteousness? How can you trust His goodness? As you get to know the names of God and understand their meaning, God's character will become real to you in life-changing ways. God only revealed His names as we needed them. God is a God of depth and He has so many layers. However, even though He is unsearchable as the Bible tells us, He's not unknowable. And we know Him by the names that He used to describe His self. God only gave His children a new name as we needed to know it.

- Elohim: The All-Powerful Creator
- Jehovah: The Self-Revealing One
- Adonai: The Owner of All
- Jehovah-Jireh: The Lord Who Provides
- Jehovah-Tsaba: The Lord Our Warrior
- El Shaddai: The Almighty Sufficient One
- El Elion: The Most High Ruler
- Jehovah Nissi: The Lord's Banner of Victory
- Jehovah Shalom: The Lord Our Peace
- Jehovah Mekadesh: The Lord Who Sanctifies
- Jehovah Rophe: The Lord Who Heals
- Jehovah Tsikenu: The Lord My Righteousness
- Jehovah Rohi: The Lord My Shepherd
- Immanuel: God With Us

By studying and understanding the characteristics of God as revealed through His names, you become better equipped to face hardship and victory, loss and provision, and all of the challenges life throws at you. Whatever name that God has revealed to us we can expect Him to live up to it. If He has revealed Himself to you as Jehovah Rophe, the God who heals, you can expect Him to live up to His name. If He has revealed Himself to you as Jehovah Shalom, you can expect Him to live up to His name.

Today I want you to realize that you are powerless over other people's expectations of you. The most important expectation is your heavenly father's and after that your own expectation of yourself. So think positive, good, and powerful thoughts, especially concerning yourself. Evict all negative thoughts. Stop allowing negative thoughts to occupy space in your mind. You wouldn't let someone that's not family to live in your house without paying rent right? So stop allowing negative thoughts to occupy space in your mind without paying rent.

Any thoughts that don't benefit you and that don't make you feel loved; these are the thoughts that need to be evicted. Because, if you can control your mind you can control your life. This goes for the kind of music that you listen to as well. Music is so powerful that it is one of the only things that can get into your spirit without your permission and we must remember that lucifer was the chief musician in Heaven. That's why you can come out of a high and oily service speaking in tongues, with the praises of God on your lips. But as soon as a car with a bumping system drives by playing a catchy beat, you'll start nodding your head or tapping your feet. As soon as the beat of Michael Jackson's "Billy Jean" hits the atmosphere even the Bishop of Canterbury starts nodding his head. That's a joke beloved, it's okay to laugh.

And satan uses music to program people to do and act in a way that they wouldn't normally act. And this is why you will see nice church girls start twerking and dropping it like it's hot as soon as certain music has entered the atmosphere. You can't listen to Cardi B. talking about how she sexually satisfies her man or men or Beyonce talking about using the Bible as tampons along with the demonic beat that was given to them from satan himself and then go back to singing, "I know it was the blood, I know it was the blood for me...." There will be some disingenuousness going on somewhere, that's for sure. So protect your eyegate, your eargate, your skingate (touch), your nosegate, and your mouthgate (taste and speech), because the enemy comes in and defeats us through our senses.

And how you respond to other people's expectations and needs of you will affect the course of your life. You were born looking like your daddy, but you will die looking like your decisions. So choose God, choose wisely, and please while you're at it, choose yourself.

Philippians 1:6 (NKJV)

⁶ being confident of this very thing, that He who has begun a good work in you will complete it until the day of Jesus Christ;

The sexiest feature of a woman, in my opinion, is her confidence. I know and have met women that does not have the Meagan Good, Halle Berry, or Sanaa Lathan type of beauty in the face, or the voluptuous body of a Angela Bassett, Dolly Parton or a Kim Kardashian, but exudes every bit of beauty and "sexy" in their walk, talk, sitting, standing, dressing, ambition, and even mindset. And what pulls it off for these women is their confidence.

I have known many drop dead gorgeous women who didn't believe that they were physically or spiritually and it always made them much less attractive. You have to know who you are beloved. Because your energy enters the room before you do. Some people come into the room and drain all of the energy out of the room with their negativity or complaining or otherwise. Some people come into the room and brightens it with their joy, their spirit, and their countenance.

Your perception of yourself affects your vibe. So make sure that you love yourself. And also be confident in your looks, because God gave them to you, you didn't. So keep working on yourself inside and outside. Stay in the Word, go to church, pray, and oh yeah, hit that gym. You got this beloved. The force is with you so just continue to express your talents and spiritual gifts and allow the good vibes to flow.

Tough Love

Faith deals with invisibles, but love that is invisible ain't love.

Apostle Dr. Larry Birchett, Jr.

Romans 12:9-10 (NKJV)

⁹Let love be without hypocrisy. Abhor what is evil. Cling to what is good. ¹⁰Be kindly affectionate to one another with brotherly love, in honor giving preference to one another;

John Lennon, a famous Singer for the world acclaimed singing group called the Beatles, once said during his interview with an American Magazine, that: 'Christianity will end, it will disappear. I do not have to argue about that.. I am certain.' He went on to say, 'Jesus was ok, but his subjects were too simple, today we are more famous than Him'. This was said in the year 1966. Lennon, **after** saying that the Beatles were more famous than Jesus Christ, was shot six times.

Tancredo Neves, was the President-elect of Brazil in the year 1985. During the Presidential campaign, he said if he got 500,000 votes from his party, not even God would remove him from Presidency.

Sure he got the votes, but he got sick a day before being made President, then he died. The New York Times headlines read, "Brazil's Leader Dies At Age 75; Never Sworn In."

Cazuza, was a Bi-sexual Brazilian composer, singer and poet. During A show in Canecio, Rio de Janeiro, while smoking his cigarette, he puffed out some smoke into the air and said: 'God, that's for you.' He died at the age of 32 of **Lung Cancer** in a horrible manner.

After the construction of Titanic, a reporter asked the man who constructed the Titanic, how safe the Titanic would be. With an ironic tone he said, 'Not even God can sink it'. What do you think happened beloved? Yep, you guessed it, the Titanic was sunk on its maiden voyage by an iceberg that was big enough and strong enough to damage it to the point of sinking it.

Marilyn Monroe, a legendary Actress, Singer and sex symbol, was visited by Billy Graham during a presentation of a show. He said the Spirit of God had sent him to preach to her. After hearing what the Preacher had to say, she said, 'I don't need your Jesus'. A week later, she was found dead in her apartment.

Marilyn was married at the age of 16 to her first husband, Jimmy Dougherty. According to the bio on Monroe's official web site, Dougherty, said of his wife, "She was a sweet, generous and religious girl." Marilyn Monroe was reared as a foster child in a devoutly Christian family in Hawthorne, California but there is not much information about what her spiritual beliefs were before she died except for information provided to us by Evangelist Billy Graham. Monroe's death was ruled to be "acute barbiturate poisoning" by Los Angeles County Coroner, Dr. Thomas Noguchi. And apparently she did need our Jesus.

I could go on and on with these kind of stories exemplifying the fact that many people thought that they didn't need our Jesus or that they were the masters of their own fate, the captains of their own lives. But time and time again, God has allowed them to eat their own words. The Bible says it this way:

Galatians 6:7-9 (KJV)

⁷ Be not deceived; God is not mocked: for whatsoever a man soweth, that shall he also reap.

⁸ For he that soweth to his flesh shall of the flesh reap corruption; but he that soweth to the Spirit shall of the Spirit reap life everlasting.

⁹ And let us not be weary in well doing: for in due season we shall reap, if we faint not.

The bible tells us in 1 Corinthians 13 that love is not puffed up and does not act unseemingly. And if you are a person that constantly rails against God, the people of God, and the things of God, you don't love Him. It's really that simple.

Telling someone the truth is not hate, it's love. Too many people in our generation label love as hate and hate as love and of course that's exactly what satan wants. It's one of his greatest tricks. We get so touchy when someone tells us about ourselves. All of the people that I just listed above was warned about God and the acceptance of Jesus one more time. They were given at least one more chance. Marilyn Monroe, for example, probably took Evangelist Billy Graham's approach as being pushy or religious or too aggressive. But I guarantee that it was the Spirit of God that spurred Billy Graham to give Marilyn Monroe one more chance to make the decision to return to the Lord. She rejected him and was dead within one week.

Tough love is the form of love that some people need. Because for a lot of people if it doesn't hurt them it doesn't change them. God used tough love to turn Saul who would later be called Paul. Some people have to feel it to make a shift.

Too many people use the "If I can't see it, I won't believe it." But the truth is that we can see God. We see Him through His love.

Seeing God Through Love

1 John 4:12-16 (NKJV)

[12] No one has seen God at any time. If we love one another, God abides in us, and His love has been perfected in us. [13] By this we know that we abide in Him, and He in us, because He has given us of His Spirit. [14] And we have seen and testify that the Father has sent the Son as Savior of the world. [15] Whoever confesses that Jesus is the Son of God, God abides in him, and he in God. [16] And we have known and believed the love that God has for us. God is love, and he who abides in love abides in God, and God in him

And so this particular text tells us that if we love one another, God abides in us and His love is perfected in us. So when we're loving correctly then people are experiencing God through us, because He's in us and His love has been perfected in us. When we are operating in the agape love of God we may be the only God that a person has ever met. This is a huge responsibility but this is a great privilege. That's why we can't go around mad at the world. We have to resolve to not allow things to ruffle our feathers and get us flustered so fast.

It's time to grow up and maturity is required to find love and to live your best life. So stop whining about who's helping you or not helping you and stop complaining about who is for you or not for you. Just know that Romans 8:31 is still valid.

Romans 8:31 (KJV)

[31] What shall we then say to these things? If God be for us, who can be against us?

As we have already went over in prior chapters our words shape our lives and they also expose who we are in our heart. Fresh water and bitter water can't come out of the same spout. So if you claim to love God, your significant other, your children, or whoever and whatever, you can't mock them from the same mouth and expect the other person to feel loved. The truth of this concept is how Delilah, an unGodly Philistine woman, finally convinced Samson to divulge his heavenly secret.

Judges 16:15-18 (Berean Study Bible)

15"How can you say, 'I love you,' " she asked, "when your heart is not with me? This is the third time you have mocked me and failed to reveal to me the source of your great strength!"

16Finally, after she had pressed him daily with her words and pleaded until he was sick to death, 17Samson told her all that was in his heart: "My hair has never been cut, because I have been a Nazirite to God from my mother's womb. If I am shaved, my strength will leave me, and I will become as weak as any other man."

18When Delilah realized that he had revealed to her all that was in his heart, she sent this message to the lords of the Philistines: "Come up once more, for he has revealed to me all that is in his heart." Then the lords of the Philistines came to her, bringing the money in their hands.

Even the world knows that you can't lie to, deceive, put down or mock a person, place, or thing that you're supposed to love and pretend that your love is genuine. So why do we as Christians think that we will be guiltless against God concerning this?

Love is more about action and doing than anything else. Our Christian walk is about surrendering ourselves to the will of God as He perfects us by making us more like Him. Perfection is a gradual process that we will only fully come into when we leave this Earth and join God in Heaven.

Sloppy Agape

Too many of us operate under the guise of what I like to call "sloppy agape" and walk around as if we are the best thing since slice bread. Sloppy agape is when you know how to give good love and you don't. You become sloppy with it. Sloppy agape is when you take what God has given you for granted. And a lot of people do this when they become unhappy vertically or horizontally. Meaning many people get mad at God or with someone else relationally for example.

Like for example when you know that you should buy flowers for your wife sometimes for no reason at all but you don't. Or when you should tell the person you love, that you actually love them before you hang up the phone, but you don't. That's sloppy agape. Or maybe when you should give your wife or husband or son or daughter a kiss before you leave the house but you don't. That's sloppy agape. Or how about when you deprive your wife or husband from sex for way too long and expecting them to feel totally and completely loved? That's sloppy agape. Laying in the bed with an old night gown and rollers in your head is sloppy agape ladies. Especially if your upset that your man is not showing you enough attention.

And a public service announcement to my men. Allowing your stomach and back fat to hang over your belt is not sexy to any woman. Get yourself in shape because yes, it matters. Don't let anyone tell you any different. Or how about when you forget your anniversary but remember other people's special moments? That's sloppy agape. Or how about when it's a special moment or day for you and your loved one and you forget to get the flowers and you decide to do McDonalds or something on that level instead of taking your lady somewhere nice. That's sloppy agape men and in my book that's not agape at all. When you love someone it brings you joy to bring them joy and to see them happy.

We can go deeper because sloppy agape can apply to supposed Godly things as well. For example, when you have time for everything that the "church" is doing but you have no time for your husband or wife, this is a distortion of what serving God really is supposed to mean or be like. Or when you call the preacher or pastor "Sir" or "Ma'am" and treat them special but don't treat your spouse the same or better. How many of you know that this is very sloppy and makes the "Church" and God for that matter, look bad? And we shouldn't expect our spouses or children for this matter, to feel loved and special if we operate like this because this is not the way that God intended us to operate. The order of things should always be God first, family second, and then ministry.

The world's way of loving is a "because" sort of love. I love you *because* I feel love for you. I love you *because* of what I get out of it. I love you *because* you're so loveable and beautiful, not to mention that you're nice to me.

But that's not how God loves us. The apostle John said, *"We love because he first loved us."* (1 John 4:19). God loved us first, even when that love wasn't being returned. God's love is not a "because" sort of love, but a "just because" sort of love. It's who God is. "God is *agape*" John said (1 John 4:16). It's the essence of his being.

Because of this, "agape" is self-giving, not self-serving. It doesn't come with conditions attached to it. And it's sacrificial in nature, because the one offering it gives, *just because.* Whether they get anything in return from it or not. Whether you're mad at them or not. Whether they make you happy or not. Whether they're your favorite person at the moment or not. We should always operate in love, even if it's only for loves sake.

One thing that I've learned from being a Soldier for almost two decades, and an athlete way before that in the sports of basketball and boxing is that effort can't be coached. It can be discussed but it can't be coached. You can coach talent and other things related to athleticism but you should never have to coach effort anyway. The more desire you have for someone or something the more effort you will apply.

Some people are more naturally gifted than you physically on a basketball court or in a boxing ring, but it doesn't mean that they should outwork you. They should never outwork you. They should never give more effort than you. And that same lesson should apply to love and being loved. Whatever you do, do it from love, not for love.

Our spouses, children, and significant others are secretly unhappy because we're not putting the maximum effort that we can put into our relationship with them. We know that we can do better but we choose not to because of ungratefulness, ego, and laziness. We're not flexing, in fact we're actually taking love for granted and reaping something average.

I was asked a question one time by somebody that was interested in me romantically many years ago. Her question to me was, "Do you love your wife?" Of course I said yes. So she said, "Does she love you?" Of course I said, yeah. Her next statement was something that has stayed with me ever since she said it. Her words were, "I can love you way better than she ever has loved you." I tried to joke with her. I said, "Girl, that ain't cute...lol. You're so rude. You need to stop." And I said all of that very lighthearted and laughingly. And then she said, "I'm serious. If I had a man like you, he'd be the luckiest man on the planet, because I'd spoil you in ways that I can tell that you're not." Once she said that, I knew I had to put her in her place and explain to her that she never met my wife and I also let her know that I really loved my wife and that I'm very happy. I ended it with, please don't ever disrespect her like that again, because that wasn't cool. She got the point and she calmed down. This was my military days. And later on in this particular tour of training, I had to shut this young woman down completely. Some spirits you have to tell it to get thee behind thee and keep on moving beloved.

I recounted this story because if I did not truly love my wife, this pressure and unknown temptation to her that I was enduring, could've ended up totally different. The point of interest that she was proposing to me was that I may be in love and I may think that my wife loves me, but that her love wasn't good enough. That she could love me better. The enemy through the woman had introduced to me the concept of "good love". satan was coming at me proposing that the love that I was enjoying with my wife was stale, boring, and inadequate. It wasn't good enough; is what he wanted me to surmise. But I praise God that I was able to use the Word of God in the situation. Because I remember stating Proverbs 18:22 along with other scriptures to the chick:

Proverbs 18:22 (KJV)

Whosoever findeth a wife, findeth a good thing, and obtain favor from the Lord.

The late Tina Turner, wrote a hit song many years ago called, 'What's Love Got To Do With It'. Answer: Everything. Love is an action word and when our actions are motivated by love, the results are positive and powerful. Love changes everything. Love makes a house a home and changes normal mundane things into the memories that keep you going for the rest of your life. Love makes you stay married for better or worse, richer or poorer, and in sickness and health. What kind of love would make you endure through all of these situations? The answer is good love.

Good Love

One of my favorite songs in the entire world is **You Give Good Love** by Whitney Houston. The meat of the lyrics go like this:

I found out what I've been missing
Always on the run
I've been looking for someone

Now you're here like you've been before
And you know just what I need
It took some time for me to see

That you give good love to me, baby
So good, take this heart of mine into your hands
You give good love to me (you give good love to me)
It's never too much (never too much, will never be)
Baby, you give good love (ah)

Never stopping, I was always searching
For that perfect love
The kind that girls like me dream of

Now you're here like you've been before
And you know just what I need
It took some time for me to see

That you give good love to me, baby
It's so good, take this heart of mine into your hands
You give good love to me (you give good love to me)
It's never too much (never too much, will never be)
Baby, you give good love, ooh

Now I, I can't stop looking around
It's not what this love's all about
Our love is here to stay, to stay
Baby, you give good love

you give
(Never too much, will never be)
So good
Take this heart of mine
Into your hands
You give good love to me (you give good love to me)
Never, never too much (never too much, will never be)
No, no, no, no, no
You give good love to me (you give good love to me)
So good, so good (you give good love, baby)

I bring up the song and the lyrics of this particular song because I believe that Whitney Houston's lyrics touch on some pretty important things as it relates to love. She started out saying, "I've found out what I've been missing. Always on the run, I've been looking for someone." Too many of us find out what true love is by mistake. And the problem is that we don't know what we're looking for because we've never seen the genuine article. We could be living in a city made of gold, a house made of diamonds, with the most Godly and most attentive spouse. But if we've never seen gold, or know the worth of diamonds and have a reverence for God's ways and methods it won't mean a thing. And the problem is that the enemy has made many to think this very thing. And he started this in the Garden of Eden. He said to Eve, "Has God said?" and then he went on to downplay God's words and change its meanings and Eve was deceived.

Don't let the enemy deceive you beloved. Real love, healthy love, safe love, true love, and most of all Godly love, does exist. And you don't have to settle for toxic, dysfunctional, unsafe, and ungodly love ever again. Too many of us engage in relationships that mimic what we saw either in real life or on television thinking that those examples had to be how it was supposed to go in real life. I'm not speaking from theory, I'm speaking from experience. And the danger of this is that you'll wind up with the same results of the wrong forms of love that you think that you're supposed to emulate.

Truth is that hurt people hurt people. And a lot of our examples of marriage or so-called Godly relationships were modeled by people that had been hurt and never healed as well. The odds are that your mother and father were operating according to the warp examples that they had seen growing up and their parents did the same and their grandparents did the same and on and on and on. It becomes the generational curse that the enemy would love to keep propagating until the end of time. But the Bible says in Proverbs 6:31 that when the thief is found, he must restore.

Proverbs 6:31 (NKJV)

31 Yet when he is found, he must restore sevenfold;
He may have to give up all the substance of his house.

And I pray that as we exposing the works of the enemy is this body of work that God will restore unto you everything that the cankerworm, locust, and palmerworm have eaten beloved, sevenfold.

We have to understand that God works in Seasons but satan, our enemy works in cycles. And he would love to keep you and I going through cycle after cycle after cycle. So when you see certain cycles keep occurring in your life, you know that it's time to start conducting spiritual warfare against the enemy. You have to decree and declare that the devil is a liar and every work of the enemy must cease and desist in your life right now in Jesus mighty name. The power of the Holy Spirit working through prayer is what can and will break every generational curse in your life.

Your scars are what make you what you are. It is not intended for you to remove them or to go back and change them. Live with them and just don't allow your defeats to become your identity. Stop allowing your defeats to define you. Learn how to allow your failures fertilize your future. A friend of mine shared something one day and I loved it. I'm going to share it with you in bullet form with a little commentary. It's called "The Five W's of Life."

THE FIVE W's of Life

1. WHO you are is what makes you special. Don't change for no one.

2 WHAT lies ahead WILL ALWAYS BE A MYSTERY. Don't be afraid to explore.

- There is always more than one choice to be made. The key is to ask God for grace to make the correct decision.

- You weren't made to play it safe, you were made to play.

- I believe that God delights in those of us that are not afraid to ask for a hard thing. God is sitting up there in Heaven saying, the sky is the limit.

- Two scripture references that I'd like to throw in this outline to show how great God wants to bless us is Ephesians 3:20 and James 4:1-6.

Ephesians 3:20 (NKJV)

[20]*Now to Him who is able to do exceedingly abundantly above all that we ask or think, according to the power that works in us, [21]to Him be glory in the church by Christ Jesus to all generations, forever and ever. Amen.*

James 4:1-6 (NKJV) Pride Promotes Strife

*<u>1</u>Where do wars and fights come from among you?
Do they not come from your desires for pleasure that war in your members?*

<u>2</u>You lust and do not have. You murder and covet and cannot obtain. You fight and war. ***Yet you do not have because you do not ask.***

<u>3</u>You ask and do not receive, because you ask amiss, that you may spend it on your pleasures.

<u>4</u>Adulterers and adulteresses! Do you not know that friendship with the world is enmity with God? Whoever therefore wants to be a friend of the world makes himself an enemy of God.

<u>5</u>Or do you think that the Scripture says in vain, "The Spirit who dwells in us yearns jealously"?

<u>6</u>But He gives more grace. Therefore He says: "God resists the proud, But gives grace to the humble."

3. **WHEN life pushes you over, you push back HARDER.**

4. **WHERE there are choices to make, choose the one that you WON'T REGRET.**

    - This goes for business, personal, private, public, and even your personal relationships.

    - You have to set your relationship goals so high that it'd be impossible for you to achieve them on your own. I mean set them so high that you're going to need God

Himself to make you and that person to fly to meet them. If you get anywhere close to flying with somebody, that person just might be the one. (the problem is that some of you set the bar too low. They take you to McDonalds and you ready to get married...lol)

5. **WHY things happen will NEVER be certain** (while you're here on Earth). Take it in stride and move forward.

- Even if this is your second or third or umpteenth time at a successful relationship, successful business, successful physical health, mental health, spiritual health, DON'T GIVE UP. Scripture tells us to be cast down but not destroyed.

Some people come into your life knowing that they're broken. Some people's toxic trait is that they know that a piece of them is still broken. And that's why they don't trust you when you say that you're going to stay and be loyal. Because of piece of them is still broken. And deep down they love it when you love them from a distance because they know that you will never really see the real them. They can hide because of you're not personal enough is what I'm saying. These type of people love when the love is not as intimate as it should be because then they can hide behind the shame of their brokenness hoping that you will never discover that they're not complete within themselves.

Some people laugh to keep from crying. And some spend just as much time getting high or drunk to live in any reality that it is other than the real one.

A lot of these issues and more stem from broken people and broken spirits. And that's why it takes time to get to know a person and if they are worth the time that it requires to really know if they are in fact your person. *Guard your heart because from it, flows the issues of life.*

I've already shared in this book that for my wife and I it took less than a year, but I never prescribe this time period to others. Because for my wife and I God was in it and we were following God's commands for many others they are led by their flesh. If you're led by your flesh the end is not going to be nice beloved. If you don't take the necessary time then you will wind up having a threesome with the other person's depression and anxiety issues. The root of both are spiritual.

The scripture tells us in Philippians 4 to not be anxious for anything but everything in prayer with supplication and thanksgiving we are to make our request known to God and the peace of God that surpass all understanding will fill our hearts and minds through Christ Jesus. Stay prayed up and ask God what His will for your next move is.

When you think about your future, do you see obstacles or possibilities? If you see obstacles, then you need to get your eyes checked and possibly get a vision alignment. I wear glasses at this point of my life. But I went through a whole 19 year military career without wearing glasses. The funny thing is that as soon as I became officially separated from the US Army, I started having issues with my sight. I can remember preaching and teaching on one Sunday and I started struggling with reading the words out of the Bible and the printed sermon and one of our members screamed out, "Pastor you need glasses". As you can imagine, I was embarrassed. Not because the parishioner yelled out, but because the parishioner was correct.

Life is sometimes like this. We go about doing things a certain way because it's the way that we've always done it. There are signs that something is different, that something needs to change. But because we are comfortable in the way that things are and have always been we go about things the way that we've always gone about things. Some of us refuse to be uncomfortable even to the point of denial, until we can no longer deny that something needs to change.

Just as in my case with needing glasses, sometimes other people can see things in our lives that we can't see until someone else points it out. Seeing who you are, unapologetically and unfiltered is important. Because we are a product of who we think we are. We gauge who we think we are by what we see, concerning ourselves. Because if you see it, you can be it.

That's why it takes generations for certain bloodlines to break out of poverty stricken experiences and do something really extraordinary with their lives. They had to see the first person graduate from college in the family! Some of you are first generation graduates in your family I'm sure. And they had to see you accomplish these things first to believe that they can do it too.

They had to see you become the first dentist. They had to see you become the first medical doctor. They had to see the first theological doctor. They had to see you become the first military officer. They had to see you become the first pastor in the family.

Point being, that sometimes if we can't see it, we won't believe that we can be it. And that's the reason why you had to go through that job layoff. And that's why you had to go through that daddy or mommy abandonment. And that's why God allowed the divorce in your life. Because he had to show you that you will go through some tough times in this life but He will never leave you nor forsake you!

I've seen a lot of things in my life but I've never seen the righteous forsaken, nor his seed begging bread. And I'm here to let you know that there is no failure in God. Defeat is simply not an option when it comes to God. We will only win when we stay in the things of God. God's will ultimately is always done in Heaven and on Earth. And this goes for the good things that we will do in His name as well.

Ephesians 2:10 (KJV)

For we are his workmanship, created in Christ Jesus unto good works, which God hath before ordained that we should walk in them.

This scripture is saying a lot but the key word is walk. It doesn't say that we have to run. Paul is saying all we have to do is walk, because direction is more important than speed. It's not a race, run at your own pace but just keep going in the right direction.

What good is it if you're going the fastest but to a dead end or an early death or worse to Hell? Stay on the right path beloved and eventually you will arrive at the place of your purpose. Run in your **own lane, at your own pace, because you are running your own race.**

It's silly to run in someone else's lane anyway. When you're running in someone else's lane you have to run at their pace and run their race. And you know what's even worse than running in someone else's lane? Allowing other people to run in yours. God has prepared lanes for all of us, so don't think you're being Godly when you allow someone else to get in front of your "work" that Ephesians 2:10 is referring to. Remember, run in your own lane, at your own pace, because it's your race.

Simply put, stop allowing people to hitchhike off of your anointing. Tell them to go get their own. Tell them, "Hey, I paid for mines and it wasn't cheap baby." Wisdom is the principal thing beloved and letting someone else run in your lane, especially right in front of you is not wisdom. It's stupid. Especially when we put these people in front of us. If we were smart we would at least put them behind us, right? And we wonder why we are not advancing.

We have to use wisdom in this season of our lives. Wisdom is the principal thing. Just because we have history, don't mean that we have a destiny. Just because you were in my past don't mean that you have to be in my future.

Most of us don't understand how important wisdom is in every part of our life. In the Book of Enoch, chapter 32, Enoch is told by the angel Raphael, that the tree that Adam and Eve ate from, titled as the Tree of the Knowledge of Good and Evil in the book of Genesis, was actually the Tree of Wisdom.

Enoch 32:6

[6] I said: 'How beautiful is the tree, and how attractive is its look!' Then Raphael the holy angel, who was with me, answered me and said: 'This is the tree of wisdom, of which thy father old (in years) and thy aged mother, who were before thee, have eaten, and they learnt wisdom and their eyes were opened, and they knew that they were naked and they were driven out of the garden.'
Refer to (Génesis 2:8-9), (Génesis 2:16-17), (Génesis 3:2-7)

Also let's look at Proverbs as it pertain to wisdom and it's relation to a relationship between a husband and a wife.

(Proverbs 3:13, 18)

"[13] Happy is the man who finds wisdom, And the man who gains understanding;
[18] She is a tree of life to those who take hold of her, And happy are all who retain her."

In order to find wisdom as Prov. 3:13 states, you have to be able to see it when it presents itself. Somebody say, "God correct my vision!" And now that you can see through the lens of the Holy Spirit, somebody needs to start telling that devil to get out of my way. Low self-esteem, get out of my way! Abandonment and abuse issues, get out of my way! Lust, get out of my way! Anger, get out of my way! Depression, get out of my way! Suicide, get out of my way! The blood of Jesus is against you!

Philippians 3:14-15 (King James Version)

[14] I press toward the mark for the prize of the high calling of God in Christ Jesus.

[15] Let us therefore, as many as be perfect, be thus minded: and if in anything ye be otherwise minded, God shall reveal even this unto you.

Long live the rose that grew from concrete when no one else even care beloved. Because you are that rose. All the hell that you've been through in your life. All of the trauma that you've lived through. All of the abuse that you had to survive through. You were and are that rose that was planted in concrete but still bloomed anyway. I guarantee you that the only one who always cared was God. Give Him praise for that somebody!

Hebrews 12:1-2 (King James Version)

*[12] Wherefore seeing we also are compassed about with so great a cloud of witnesses, let us lay aside every weight, **and the sin** which doth so easily beset us, and let us run with **patience** the race that is **set before us,***

*[2] **Looking unto Jesus** the author and finisher of our faith; who for the joy that was set before him endured the cross, despising the shame, and is set down at the right hand of the throne of God.*

Too many of us are looking at the way that God moved yesterday instead of focusing on how God is moving today. You will never be defeated if you allow God to move differently for and in you in this season.

Isaiah 43:19 (King James Version)

[19] Behold, I will do a new thing; now it shall spring forth; shall ye not know it? I will even make a way in the wilderness, and rivers in the desert.

The Power of Connection

We accept the love that we think we deserve.

Apostle Dr. Larry Birchett, Jr.

Ephesians 5:25-26 (KJV)

[25] Husbands, love your wives, just as Christ loved the church and gave himself up for her [26] to make her holy, cleansing her by the washing with water through the word.

I want to end this body of work talking about power of connection. Because connection is why we're here. It's what gives purpose and meaning to our lives. If you show me your five closest connections that you interact with on a daily basis, I can tell you who and what you are. The most important connection besides our connection to God is marriage. Because it exemplifies the greatest love that a person can experience on Earth besides the love of God to us. The marriage union is representative of our relationship with Jesus Christ. Christ is the groom, we are His bride. And how loyal we are to our spouse is a direct correlation to how faithful we are to God. The Bible is clear in that there is no greater love that we can have for a person than to lay our life down for them. Jesus did that for us and showed us, not just told us, that His love for us is unconditional.

The truth of the matter is that unless Jesus is enough for you, NO man, woman, occupation, career, ministry or otherwise will be enough for you. So, besides our vertical love for God through Christ the next best gift of love that God has given us is the power of an intimate covenantal relationship, which normally manifests into what we call marriage.

God looked at Adam in the Garden of Eden and said that it's not good for man to be alone. And so He put Adam to sleep and conducted the first surgery on mankind and took a rib out of Adam and made Eve. Adam was the only human created. Eve and every one else was birthed or recreated from another person. And God decided that Adam and every human being would be better off with a companion. God deemed early on in creation that we are better when we are connected to someone else. Why? Because, connection gives you power. Connection gives you power. Attachment sucks the life out of you.

A lot of relationship experts and doctors and philosophers will tell you that Communication is the most important component of an intimate covenantal relationship. But that's not true, connection is. Communication is important and it's high on the list. But communication is merely an exchange of information, while connection is an exchange of our humanity and on a deeper lever, our spirit. This is why I stated early in this book that if the "love" is not organic, it's not love. I can talk to probably 20 or 30 females for hours and hours probably better than I can talk to my wife when it comes to tone and politeness and other semantics involved in conversation. But I can guarantee you that I don't have that same spark, that same connection that I have with my wife. Because she and only she is my soulmate. She and only she is the woman that I'm in covenant with before God and it's not a superficial thing, our souls are connected.

I love the picture that is given to us in the book of love that's included in the Bible called the Song of Solomon. Song of Solomon is the steamiest book in the Bible when it comes to love and romance and even sex. Let's look at a few verses in Song of Solomon, chapter 3.

Song of Solomon 3: 1-7 (KJV)

[1]*By night on my bed I sought him whom my soul loveth: I sought him, but I found him not.* [2]*I will rise now, and go about the city in the streets, and in the broad ways I will seek him whom my soul loveth: I sought him, but I found him not.* [3]*The watchmen that go about the city found me:* to whom I said, *Saw ye him whom my soul loveth?* [4] **It was but a little that I passed from them, but I found him whom my soul loveth: I held him, and would not let him go, until I had brought him into my mother's house, and into the chamber of her that conceived me.** [5]*I charge you, O ye daughters of Jerusalem, by the roes, and by the hinds of the field, that ye stir not up, nor awake* my *love, till he please.* [6]*Who* is *this that cometh out of the wilderness like pillars of smoke, perfumed with myrrh and frankincense, with all powders of the merchant?* [7]*Behold his bed,* which is *Solomon's; threescore valiant men* are *about it, of the valiant of Israel.*

My wife and I have a plaque of Song of Solomon 3:4 over our bed to remind us that we are not just friends, buddies, old pals, we are soulmates. To remind us that out of the 7 billion humans that are living on the Earth that God allowed us to find each other. He had to bring my wife from another country, Jamaica. And He had to make sure that we were both saved and serving Him first. And He had to set it up that we would be in the same service, in the same church, in Philadelphia, on the right night, after a lot of failed relationships had taken place on both sides, so that we can see and recognize each other. It's mind boggling and amazing. But like the old adage says, when you find the right one, you will understand why all of the other ones didn't work out.

Connection is not just good communication. Connection is the energy that exists between people when they feel seen, heard, and valued. It exists when two people can give and receive without judgment. And it thrives when these same people can derive sustenance and are strengthened by the relationship.

John Lennon said, "A dream you dream alone is only a dream. A dream you dream together is reality."

If there is no covenant there is no God in it. God designed marriage to be a committed covenant relationship between a man and a woman. This is what separates an attachment from a connection. There is power in connection not attachment. Attachment to a tribe or a group is great but it does not top the intimacy of connection. There is no covenant in boyfriend and girlfriend level. There is no permanent covenant in friend or best friend level. But there is covenant, normally sealed by blood when we're talking in the biblical sense when we refer to marriage. **Now, the key word to the definition of marriage is covenant.** If there is no covenant, then there is no union.

God's original thought to the best state of mankind is seen in the very first book of the Bible.

Genesis 2:18 (NLT)

Then the Lord God said, "It is not good for the man to be alone. I will make a helper who is just right for him."

What we can surmise from the progression of scripture is that after He observed Adam, the first man, for a little while, He realized that even though Adam was enjoying himself in the Garden of Eden, he would really enjoy it more if he had someone to share his experiences with. Adam saw the lions connecting with other lions. He saw the birds connecting with other birds. The monkeys with other monkeys. But he in himself, saw nothing and no one in creation that he can connect to. Likewise, when we consider the power of two, as it relates to marriage, it undoubtedly is one of the most beautiful expressions of God's love in existence. Because again, marriage is the expression of God in the Earth.

One of the clearest scriptures in the Bible regarding who and what God is

1 John 4:7-8 (ESV):

⁷Beloved, let us love one another, for love is from God, and whoever loves has been born of God and knows God. ⁸Anyone who does not love does not know God, because God is love.

These scriptures let us know that God in His purest essence is love. The Bible also teaches us that He created us for His pleasure and that He loves us. The meaning of life is love. Therefore, the greatest gift in life is love. One of the greatest expressions of love in this Earth is the institution of marriage, of which, God Himself, created in the Garden of Eden when He said that *it is not good for man to be alone.*

The interesting thing about marriage is that not everyone is designed or destined for it. And we see that clearly in Paul's teaching in **1 Corinthians 7:7-9**, where he is basically exhorting every single person to stay to themselves like he was unless they were burning with passion toward someone else. Which is sobering and makes us understand that marriage is really a special gift from God to be cherished and relished, because it means that before the creation of the world God destined for you to experience this gift of love with someone else of the opposite sex. It is also a calling and if you're not being called to it you should stay away from it. Why? Because the key ingredient to marriage is love.

The key ingredient to building a love that will last is the strong foundation of friendship. Too many people claim to be in love with people that they are not even friends with. This is especially the case to those individuals that have skipped the friendship or courting stage and went right to intimacy. The problem with this, besides the obvious fact that it is a sin to engage in any sexual activity before marriage, is that you can have wild and amazing sex with anyone, and not be in love with them. So, the discipline of waiting until marriage and only having sex in the sanctity of marriage **(1 Cor. 6:18; Exodus 20:14)**, as God commands us in His Word, simply protects us from making these mistakes. The trick of the enemy is to convince you that God is trying to keep you away from something. Which is not the case.

It is not the lack of love but a lack of friendship that makes unhappy marriages.
Fiedrich Nietze

Proverbs 18:22 (NLT)

*The man who finds a wife **finds a treasure**, and he **receives favor** from the Lord.*

The Bible says he who finds a wife finds a good thing, not a good marriage! Guess what? **You don't find great marriages, you build one.**

Disclaimer: God's Word exhorts us to be wise about our expectations for marriage and wise about whom we let into our hearts.

Proverbs 4:23 (KJV)

Above all else, guard your heart, for it is the wellspring of life.

Besides the obvious reason of not having your heart broken repeatedly by people that are not serious about love, we believe that when two hearts are joined together something spiritual happens that gives us more favor, power, and influence in the Earth. Remember connection creates power, attachment sucks it away. See, the Bible says that the power of life and death are in the tongue. Meaning that one person can speak things into existence and even curse some things, just like Jesus did the fig tree. However, can you imagine the power of two people totally in agreement and saying the same thing? The Bible let us know this:

Matthew 18:19-20 (NLT)

I also tell you this: If two of you agree here on earth concerning anything you ask, my Father in heaven will do it for you. For where two or three gather together as my followers, I am there among them.

Therefore, we are more powerful in the spiritual and natural, when we are joined to another person. Our prayers become more powerful because we already have another person coming into agreement with us. Our ability to create change becomes greater because now we have two people combining their resources to throw against everything that we call life. And we could go on and on regarding the benefits of two over the one, however I believe that the Bible explains biblical institutions and thoughts best. Let's look at **Ecclesiastes 4:9-12 (KJV)**:

Ecclesiastes 4:9-12 (KJV)

⁹ Two are better than one; because they have a good reward for their labour.

¹⁰ For if they fall, the one will lift up his fellow: but woe to him that is alone when he falleth; for he hath not another to help him up.

¹¹ Again, if two lie together, then they have heat: but how can one be warm alone?

¹² And if one prevail against him, two shall withstand him; and a threefold cord is not quickly broken.

Ecclesiastes 4:9-12 (NLT)

Two people are better off than one, *for they can help each other succeed. If one person falls, the other can reach out and help. But someone who falls alone is in real trouble. Likewise, two people lying close together can keep each other warm. But how can one be warm alone? A person standing alone can be attacked and defeated, but two can stand back-to-back and conquer. Three are even better, for a triple-braided cord is not easily broken.*

Think about it beloved, if you were to go on a hike wouldn't it be better to go with someone else? Especially a person that loves you more than life itself? For example, if a couple is in the wilderness together and one of them falls into a ditch. At least the person that is **not** in the ditch can help the other person out.

I want to be very clear, if there is no covenant there is no God in it. God designed marriage to be a **committed covenant relationship** between a man and a woman. **Now, the key word to the definition of marriage is covenant.** If there is no covenant, then there is no union. If there is no covenant, then technically you're still single. The covenant denotes the agreement and it doesn't add value to your life it multiplies value. Remember the scriptures say that *"one can chase one thousand, two can put ten thousand to flight."* The power of two means that the grace, power, love, resources, favor, and peace on your life will not just be added to but multiplied by the power of the Holy Spirit.

The Bible says that in order to worship God our spirit has to be aligned and **connected** to God's Spirit. Additionally, in order for the human spirit to hear from the Holy Spirit, the human spirit has to be in proximity and open to the Holy Spirit.

John 4:24 (King James Version)

²⁴ God is a Spirit: and they that worship him must worship him in spirit and in truth.

If God has blessed you with the gift of connection, you're flexing beloved. Enjoy it and protect it because you are winning and more blessed than you think you are. Watch out for the spirit of Perfection. The devil will try to make you think that unless everything is perfect, you're not doing well. I'm here to tell you that struggle has been infused in what we call life. But as long as you don't give up you will survive.

Survive the struggle man or woman of God. How do you survive? His name is Jesus! You overcome the devil by the blood of Jesus and by the testimony of how you overcame.

1 John 3:8 ………… *For this purpose the Son of God was manifested, that **HE** might destroy the works of the devil.* Watch this though: Jesus is going to beat the devil up for you and give you the credit

Revelations 12:11 *And **they** overcame him by the blood of the Lamb, and by the word of **their** testimony; and they loved not their lives unto the death.*

This scripture clearly says that "they" meaning you, will overcome him, you will overcome based on the finished work, on the victory that Jesus has already earned for you.

It does not say that God will overcome him for you, because **that has already been accomplished anyway on the Cross.** All you have to do is walk in the victory and trust the Word of God in that God has already taken care of our enemies. I love the song, **I'm A Conqueror**

(Song: I'm a conqueror, victorious, I'm reigning with Jesus, I'm seated in Heavenly places with Him, with Him. For the Kingdom of God is within me, I know, no defeat only victory. For the Kingdom of God is within me. I know no defeat only strength and power.)

Men, your wife, the woman that you are connected to is a reflection of you. She is a reflection of your energy. She is a reflection of your choice to want her to be around you. So remember that and treat her accordingly. Treat her as the Queen that she is. Remember that women are activated by love. Your connection to your wife depends on the quality of the love that you continually give her. Too many of us act as if our significant other got there by some sort of apparition. When the truth is that you pursued them. You wanted them and longed for them and asked for them to be in your life.

Women, of course the same sentiment goes for you. Because in our day and time no one knocks you over the head or force you to marry anybody that you don't want to. So treat that man as the King that he is and understand that men needs respect. Women needs love but men need respect. As a matter of fact men are drawn to respect. And this is the reason why a lot of men seem to drift away from their wife and spend more time with their friends or even sometimes with another woman. Because men are drawn to respect and if they feel like that are more respected around their friends or another woman, it's most of time because of the respect factor. It's not that they love their friends or even that little "shortie" from the job more than you, it's because they receive the respect that they were designed to receive from these third parties. Don't allow this to happen ladies. Love and respect your man like no one else on this Earth. Remember that Sarah called Abraham Lord.

Lastly, the power of two requires maturity and the ability to drop the stones.

John 8:3-11 (KJV)

³ And the scribes and Pharisees brought unto him a woman taken in adultery; and when they had set her in the midst,

⁴ They say unto him, Master, this woman was taken in adultery, in the very act.

⁵ Now Moses in the law commanded us, that such should be stoned: but what sayest thou?

⁶ This they said, tempting him, that they might have to accuse him. But Jesus stooped down, and with his finger wrote on the ground, as though he heard them not.

⁷ So when they continued asking him, he lifted up himself, and said unto them, He that is without sin among you, let him first cast a stone at her.

⁸ And again he stooped down, and wrote on the ground.

⁹ And they which heard it, being convicted by their own conscience, went out one by one, beginning at the eldest, even unto the last: and Jesus was left alone, and the woman standing in the midst.

¹⁰ When Jesus had lifted up himself, and saw none but the woman, he said unto her, Woman, where are those thine accusers? hath no man condemned thee?

¹¹ She said, No man, Lord. And Jesus said unto her, Neither do I condemn thee: go, and sin no more.

We all understand that this story is about a woman that was caught in Adultery. But the onus of Jesus response to the trap that the Pharisees was trying to trick Him to fall into was that sometimes you simply just have to drop the stones. Jesus said that whichever one of you hypocrites is without sin, cast the first stone. They all left from the oldest to the youngest. Maturity is when you can admit that **you also** have some very toxic traits. This is how you're going to keep the power of the gift of connection active in your relationship and active in your life.

Watch out for the Spirit of Jezebel. A lot of people teach it just against the women but this spirit can be found in men and women because there is a mutual submission that has to take place for a marriage to be successful.

Jezebel Spirit: Historically is a Prophetic Witch spirit. But it can be manifested in men and women. However it is mostly found in women. Jezebel is a very charismatic spirit. It is very manipulative. Always looking for a platform and uses subtle manipulation. If this is you woman, stop it. Get off of your platform and stop trying to manipulate your man or the image of your man. Men, this is beneath you but if you're operating like this, the same thing applies and you need to stop it.

The Jezebel spirit twists the scriptures. They twist the Word of God. And this is where roles are blurred, changed, and twisted. Nothing will ever change God's order of things while we are in this age. The man is the head of the woman and Christ is the head of the man. The woman is to follow the man as the man follows Christ. The man is not more special or better than the woman but he has been designed differently and created to lead and protect the weaker vessel, which is the woman, and no Jezebel spirit will ever be able to change that fact. This is Bible and as long as the man is doing it with the love of God, he is operating within his heavenly DNA.

And Jezebel will always try to assassinate your character. They always throwing darts about you behind your back. You cannot defeat Jezebel in your flesh! People who have this spirit in terms of "church" or "ministry" comes in and try to join the Intercessory

Team and the Praise and Worship Team because they are always looking for access to Altars.

Jezebel always rebel order. They never want to go through system, like classes. In marriage of course this normally translates into the wife not wanting to submit to her husband. If this is the dynamic in your marriage beloved you are not flexing you are failing.

It's embarrassing when I am around a couple that looks beautiful but are not beautiful in their dynamic to each other. I can't stand to be around them and I'm always embarrassed for the man. The Jezebel spirit always throws tantrums. Why? Because they hate submission. And likes to make it look like the other person is in error.

A man might be asked a question and the woman will barge in and answer the question before the man. Or she'll change his answer and look at him like you better not say nothing. Or is very touchy when the man is being assertive or being the Alpha like he was created to be. I'm always embarrassed for men that are in this situation. Women, if this is your issue, slow your roll, get softer, quiet yourself down a little bit and let the man be the man realizing that it takes nothing away from you. No woman is beneath any man but our roles are determined by God. And when you decide to come into covenant with a person from the opposite sex, you must remember that the covenant that you're coming into comes from the Bible, was invented and created via the Bible, and God is the founder and originator of it.

The most powerful and beautiful women that I know, know how to respect their man even in areas where they are smarter and wiser. Their husbands know it and so do we and it makes their husbands love them even more. And in most cases we all know who is "in charge" and I say that utilizing the highest intellectual privilege of what wise, seasoned and successful couples understand is true.

When I talk about this subject and everyone knowing their roles, I like to bring up music. We all love good music and a great harmony. But **music is made up of four parts: Rhythm, Beat Melody, and Harmony.** If the Rhythm tried to be the beat the music would be all messed up. If the Harmony tried to operate like the Beat, the result would be terrible. But when the Rhythm allows the Beat to be the Beat and the Melody to be the Melody and the Harmony to actually harmonize, you get beautiful music. The same thing goes with marriage. When the Husband allows the Wife to be a Wife it goes well. And when the Wife allows the Husband to be the Husband it creates a divine harmony. And all of a sudden you are Flexing beloved.

There is a fallacy going around the church that women who are strong-willed cannot be submissive in a Biblical way. But that's just not true. Marital submission is possible, even for a woman who is strong-willed.

You can find many strong-willed women who were good wives and wonderful women of God. Deborah, Queen Esther, and Ruth, are just a few that are named in the Bible.

Even the Lord Jesus Himself, had a servant's heart. And yet He was a strong leader when He needed to be. He was strong-willed, but He knew when to "lay down His life" for those He loved and be submissive. The difference is that He **knew** when it was the Father's will that He strongly exerted His position in Kingdom work, and when He was to submit. And Christ is our example. The Bible says,

"Your attitude should be the same as that of Christ Jesus: Who, being in the very nature God, did not consider equality with God something to be grasped, but made himself nothing, taking the very nature of a servant, being made in human likeness. And being found in appearance as a man, he humbled himself and became obedient to death — even death on a cross!" **(Philippians 2:5-8)**

Again, Jesus knew when to exert His strong will and when to yield to submission to God's Heavenly plan. You could in essence call Him meek. The Bible says that the "meek shall inherit the earth." When you are meek, it does not mean you have to be weak. You can be, but you don't have to be. Meekness is also defined as: "strength under control." Just because you yield when you feel it is necessary, it does not mean you are weak. As a matter of fact, it takes extra strength to yield when that is not your tendency to do so.

Someone who is meek is kind, patient, and controlled. When you are "controlled" you are not necessarily weak-willed. Those who will "inherit the earth" because they are meek, know when it is best for them to willingly step back for the betterment of the situation. They also know when to go forward in a controlled way. Meekness and voluntary submission takes true wisdom and strength of purpose and will to do this.

That's why a woman can still be strong-willed and yet be submissive when the situation calls for it. And when she is, she is Spirit-led, not led by her own self-will and determination. And the same is true with a man. Bottom line is that you reflect what you expect. And as long as you expectations are taken from the Bible your flexing. And you can't go wrong. This is why Pre-marital Counseling is important.

Our duty as Christians is to follow in Jesus' footsteps. During his life here on earth, Jesus taught us what it meant to live a truly human life as God intended for his children. Jesus taught us to love. God is love, and we are created in God's image and our command is to love. All of the commandments, summed up in Leviticus, as well as Jesus' command at the Last Supper tell us to love God and others. The more we are able to love, the closer we are to life in the Kingdom. Paul tells us in 1 Corinthians chapter 13 that all will disappear one day except for love. All that we do in love will follow us into the next world. This is what it means to die in the Lord.

You can't die in the Lord if you've never given your life to Him though beloved. One of the simplest passage of scriptures to remember to understand the process of Salvation and how to obtain it, is called The Romans Road to Salvation. It is five scriptures all from the same book. The book of Romans to be exact. And I will list them along with some commentary from myself and a Pastor Brian Tubbs who has written extensively on the Romans Road to Salvation.

"As it is written, 'There is none righteous, no, not one.'"
(Romans 3:10, KJV)

Quoting from the Psalms, the Apostle Paul declares that no single human being is "righteous" (the meaning of which is best understood as "right with God").

"For all have sinned, and come short of the glory of God." (Romans 3:23, KJV)

Lest someone protest that they are a good person, especially when compared to people they know or observe in the news or in their workplace (or wherever), Paul points out that the standard isn't your neighbor, but rather God Himself.

It isn't enough that you compare yourself to another human being and think "Well, I'm not as bad as him."

The standard is God's holiness. And all of us fall short of that standard.

"For the wages of sin is death; but the gift of God is eternal life through Jesus Christ our Lord." (Romans 6:23, KJV)

Having established that we are all sinners who fall short of God's glory, Paul explains that the "wages" (or earnings) of our sin is "death." This includes both physical death and spiritual death.

Physical death is when your soul separates from your body. Spiritual death is when your soul is separated from God. And this separation from God extends into eternity for those who die in their lost and sinful state. Don't let this be you beloved.

Because of our sin, we face the reality and inevitability of both physical death and eternal separation from God.

Paul, however, doesn't leave us with just bad news. He mentions that the "gift of God" is "eternal life through Jesus Christ our Lord." And to further explain this, we step back a chapter in Romans to go to the next milestone marker in the Romans Road.

"But God commendeth his love toward us, in that, while we were yet sinners, Christ died for us." (Romans 5:8, KJV)

God doesn't leave us in our sinful state. He doesn't leave us with the prospect of facing both physical and spiritual death. There is, as they say, "more to the story."

Paul says that God demonstrated or commended (gave) love to us even when we didn't deserve it. Even when we were deep in sin, "Christ died for us."

What do we do this information? Well, for that, we come to the final passage of the Romans Road.

"For whosoever shall call upon the name of the Lord shall be saved." (Romans 10:13, KJV)

The bad news is we all fall short of God's glory and we all face both physical and spiritual death because of it. The good news is that **God loved us, sent Jesus to die for us, and anyone who calls upon "the name of the Lord shall be saved."**

If you would like to do this right now beloved, I want to walk you through this process with a prayer. This is my version of the Sinner's Prayer. Repeat after me my brother or sister:

Father God, it's me, your child. Lord God forgive me for all of my sins, known and unknown. Lord Jesus, please come into my heart and be my Lord and personal Savior. I choose life, I reject death. I choose Heaven, I reject Hell. Please write my name in the Lambs Book of Life, with the blood of Jesus. Thank you for loving me and giving me the grace to say this prayer and mean it at this very moment in time. I love you Lord. In Jesus mighty name I pray, Amen.

If you said that prayer beloved, then I would like to be the first person to congratulate you. Welcome to the family, specifically, the Kingdom of God. You are now my brother or sister in Christ. Your next step is to find a Bible teaching and Bible believing church. Get in there and allow yourself to be developed and discipled. I am so proud of you.

The last book of the Bible is the Book of Revelations. It seems that the Book of Revelation has just as much to say to us today just as it did in the early days of the church. **We can tell if we are living in**

the Lord by the way we are living in love, and if we live in the Lord, we are more apt to die in the Lord.

Love, being the greatest force in existence and the greatest flex for every human will always be under attack. And for this reason we have to ensure that we have our armor on at all times. If you keep your armor on at all times beloved, no one will ever be able to stop you from flexing.

Ephesians 6:14–17 (ESV)

[14] Stand therefore, having fastened on the belt of truth,

and ⁵having put on the breastplate of righteousness, [15] and, as

shoes for your feet, having put on the readiness given by the gospel

of peace. [16] In all circumstances take up the shield of faith, with

which you can extinguish all the flaming darts of the evil

one; [17] and take the helmet of salvation, and the sword of the

Spirit, which is the word of God,

Keep in mind that even though this is a book about love, we need to understand that the force of love will never be able to be fully comprehended. God is love and God will never be fully comprehended by anyone or anything that He has created. And since this is the case, I think that it warranted for us to finish this book with a prayer. I love you for reading this book and there is nothing that you can do about it beloved. Keep on flexing.

PRAYER FOR TODAY: Father, I submit to You all that I am. You delivered me from the power of darkness and have brought me into the kingdom of Your dear Son, Jesus, in whom I have redemption and the forgiveness of sins through His precious blood. Thank You for Your unmerited favor and undeserved goodness upon my life. I ask that You renew my mind by the Word of God so that my thoughts are Your thoughts. Transform me into Your image I pray. In Jesus' precious name. Amen.

ABOUT THE AUTHOR

Apostle Dr. Larry Birchett, Jr., is the Founder and Senior Pastor of Harvest House Restoration Center, located in Carlisle, PA and the President of the Treasures of the Heart International Ministries that reaches across the globe. He is also the author of the acclaimed books *Reverence for the Storm, Processed for His Purpose-Purposed for His Promise, and Interdimensional Prayer*. He holds a Doctor of Ministry (DMin) from Andersonville Theological Seminary, a PhD in Counseling and Communication from Calvary's Cross Institute; an Honorary Doctorate in Humanity from Glad Tidings Institute; on top of a Master of Science in Leadership and Business Ethics (MSLBE) from Duquesne University of the Holy Spirit. Him and his wife, Prophetess Dr. Joanna Birchett, Founder of Gospel 4 U TV and Magazine Ministries and author of the acclaimed book *Defeat was Never an Option*, are trailblazers for Jesus as they pastor together and travel the world together fulfilling the Great Commission of preaching, teaching, and baptizing every soul that is assigned to the work of their hands, into the Kingdom of God.

Made in the USA
Middletown, DE
25 October 2023